The Path to the

Measuring Graduate Attrition in the Sciences and Humanities

Ad Hoc Panel on Graduate Attrition
Advisory Committee

Office of Scientific and Engineering Personnel

National Research Council

NATIONAL ACADEMY PRESS
Washington, D.C.   1996

National Academy Press • 2101 Constitution Avenue, N.W. • **Washington, D.C. 20418**

NOTICE: The project that is the subject of this report was approved by the Governing Board of the National Research Council, whose members are drawn from the councils of the National Academy of Sciences, the National Academy of Engineering, and the Institute of Medicine. The members of the committee responsible for the report were chosen for their special competences and with regard for appropriate balance.

This report has been reviewed by a group other than the authors according to procedures approved by a Report Review Committee consisting of members of the National Academy of Sciences, the National Academy of Engineering, and the Institute of Medicine.

The National Academy of Sciences is a private, nonprofit, self-perpetuating society of distinguished scholars engaged in scientific and engineering research, dedicated to the furtherance of science and technology and to their use for the general welfare. Upon the authority of the charter granted to it by the Congress in 1863, the Academy has a mandate that requires it to advise the federal government on scientific and technical matters. Dr. Bruce M. Alberts is president of the National Academy of Sciences.

The National Academy of Engineering was established in 1964, under the charter of the National Academy of Sciences, as a parallel organization of outstanding engineers. It is autonomous in its administration and in the selection of its members, sharing with the National Academy of Sciences the responsibility for advising the federal government. The National Academy of Engineering also sponsors engineering programs aimed at meeting national needs, encourages education and research, and recognizes the superior achievements of engineers. Dr. William A. Wulf is interim president of the National Academy of Engineering.

The Institute of Medicine was established in 1970 by the National Academy of Sciences to secure the services of eminent members of appropriate professions in the examination of policy matters pertaining to the health of the public. The Institute acts under the responsibility given to the National Academy of Sciences by its congressional charter to be an adviser to the federal government and, upon its own initiative, to identify issues of medical care, research, and education. Dr. Kenneth I. Shine is president of the Institute of Medicine.

The National Research Council was organized by the National Academy of Sciences in 1916 to associate the broad community of science and technology with the Academy's purposes of furthering knowledge and advising the federal government. Functioning in accordance with general policies determined by the Academy, the Council has become the principal operating agency of both the National Academy of Sciences and the National Academy of Engineering in providing services to the government, the public, and the scientific and engineering communities. The Council is administered jointly by both Academies and the Institute of Medicine. Dr. Bruce M. Alberts and Dr. William A. Wulf are chairman and interim vice chairman, respectively, of the National Research Council.

This material is based on work supported by the Andrew W. Mellon Foundation.

Library of Congress Catalog Card No. 96-67827
International Standard Book Number 0-309-05482-6

Additional copies of this report are available from:
National Academy Press
2101 Constitution Avenue, N.W.
Box 285
Washington, D.C. 20055
800-624-6242
202-334-3313 (in the Washington Metropolitan Area)
http://www.nap.edu

ACKNOWLEDGMENTS

The OSEP Advisory Committee is most grateful to Charlotte Kuh and Daniel Kleppner for their contributions to this important effort. Special acknowledgment is also extended to Pamela Flattau for formulating the charge to the ad hoc study panel and overseeing the design of the project and to Marilyn Baker for completing the report.

Much of the information presented in this report was gathered through work commissioned by the panel. Margaret E. Boeckmann and Dolores L. Burke provided helpful reviews of the literature on graduate attrition and degree completion in the fields comprising the arts and sciences. The late Betty M. Vetter and her colleagues at the Commission on Professionals in Science and Technology summarized the nature and contents of various known data bases that have been or might be used to study graduate attrition and degree completion, and George "Erik" Erikson produced a number of interesting tables to demonstrate the potential role of biographical information for enhancing our understanding of graduate preparation in the sciences and humanities.

The work of this project was conducted by the staff of the Office of Scientific and Engineering Personnel whose Executive Director, Alan Fechter, provided helpful counsel. The panel appreciates the work of Patricia Janowski, science writer, who prepared much of the material that served as the basis of this report. We are also grateful to Dimitria Satterwhite, the project's administrative assistant, and to Pamela Lohof for her editorial assistance.

Special thanks are given to Sarah E. Turner, Research Associate at the Andrew W. Mellon Foundation, whose insights contributed to the deliberations of the ad hoc study panel.

PREFACE

In 1995 doctoral degrees were granted to over 26,000 individuals in the sciences and humanities, but many other individuals who began graduate work with the same aspirations as these "completers" dropped out along the way. There are no national estimates to tell us how many students make the decision each year to cease graduate work, but studies at a few selected academic institutions suggest that as many as half the students entering certain graduate programs do not complete their doctoral degrees. Thus, it is reasonable to conclude that the nation is losing many thousands of doctoral students every year through attrition from graduate studies.

Some attrition from graduate programs is to be expected, of course, as students discover that graduate study is not for them. However, the departure of so many qualified candidates from doctoral studies represents a genuine loss of talent to society. With some further encouragement, these students might well have completed their doctorates and entered the pool of human resources that we depend upon to sustain our college and university faculties, to advance the frontiers of science and medicine, to fuel industrial development, and to generate a deeper understanding of our cultural roots.

In 1991 the Office of Scientific and Engineering Personnel, with support from the Andrew W. Mellon Foundation, asked Charlotte Kuh and Daniel Kleppner, two members of its Advisory Committee on Studies and Analyses, to serve as an ad hoc panel to summarize the existing data resources and studies on graduate attrition, with an eye to whether sufficient information is in hand to estimate the magnitude of attrition from graduate education in the sciences and humanities for the nation as a whole. Although the panel members concluded that a system to provide national estimates of attrition would be unworkable, they did identify many useful resources that should assist individual institutions in monitoring and reducing their own rates of graduate attrition.

M. R. C. Greenwood, *Chair*
OSEP Advisory Committee

CONTENTS

LIST OF TABLES

LIST OF FIGURES

EXECUTIVE SUMMARY

There is growing concern among educators and policy makers over recent levels of attrition from Ph.D. programs as reported by some U.S. universities. Of the studies currently available, some institutions place graduate attrition at 50 percent for selected fields in the sciences and humanities; others have documented attrition at levels well over 65 percent for some programs. Some attrition will always occur as students progress through demanding research degree programs. Nevertheless, the rates reported by these institutions are considered "high" compared to estimates provided by faculty and deans in 1960 when they placed attrition at 20 to 40 percent.

Our confidence in the effectiveness of graduate education in the United States depends to a large extent on the statistics that describe the outcomes of the enterprise. The estimates provided by universities today are based on careful procedures using administrative records at their institutions. Reliable estimates of graduate attrition are important because of their potential to reduce the waste inherent in the premature departure of talented individuals from advanced preparation in the sciences and humanities. Unfortunately, such estimates of graduate attrition are not available for the full complement of institutions comprising the U.S. graduate education enterprise.

This report responds to a request from the Andrew W. Mellon Foundation for a summary of data sets that could be used to monitor trends in graduate attrition and degree completion in the sciences and humanities at U.S. universities. The study was conducted under the auspices of the National Research Council's Office of Scientific and Engineering Personnel (OSEP), which invited two members of the OSEP Advisory Committee on Studies and Analyses to serve as an ad hoc panel to oversee the project.

In the course of the study the panel commissioned a summary of national data sets that have been or could be used to analyze patterns of graduate attrition and degree attainment in the sciences and humanities. The data bases are described in Appendix A of this report. The panel also commissioned two papers to identify and summarize studies of graduate attrition and degree attainment published in the past decade; these results appear in the Annotated Bibliography.

From its review of these materials, the panel concludes that there is a distinct body of knowledge about attrition from doctoral programs at U.S. universities. The panel identified three types of studies: (1) those that generated estimates of attrition utilizing administrative records, (2) those that involved special-purpose studies and surveys to document factors contributing to graduate attrition, and (3) those that modeled student persistence in graduate study.

Because of the diversity of graduate programs, however, and the need to collect data on attrition from the records of individual institutions, the panel also concludes that it is not feasible to design a system to produce national estimates of attrition from Ph.D.

programs. A few academic institutions have recently undertaken the longitudinal analyses that are needed to ascertain rates of attrition and degree attainment at their own institutions. Some movement is also evident in the educational research community to develop profiles of graduate attrition at selected groups of institutions. These studies are not expected, however, to yield national estimates of attrition from graduate studies in U.S. universities as a whole.

1

INTRODUCTION

In the twentieth century, U.S. graduate schools have changed from institutions for scholarly inquiry, largely separate from the rest of the university, to internationally preeminent institutions that are an inherent part of a university's teaching and research mission. They provide students from the United States and abroad the opportunity for advanced study in a wide variety of fields through carefully structured programs leading to the Doctor of Philosophy (Ph.D.)[1] or related research degree.

As U.S. graduate education has ascended to international preeminence, its structure and purpose have changed. Some doctoral institutions are reporting surprisingly high levels of attrition from Ph.D. programs. Attrition, though some is to be expected, has a high cost in time and resources for both students and faculty. To the extent that avoidable causes of attrition can be identified and ameliorated, graduate education can be improved.

CHANGES IN THE ACADEMIC ENVIRONMENT

The graduate school is no longer an independent institution for scholarly inquiry detached from undergraduate education as it was when doctoral programs were first established over 100 years ago at The Johns Hopkins University and Clark University (Rudolph 1962; Veysey 1970). Graduate programs are much more closely linked today to the greater utilitarian concerns that characterize contemporary university-industry-government relations (see, for example, GUIRR 1992). Significant emphasis is placed on research productivity, and faculty are often heavily engaged in research activities, sometimes at the expense of being available to graduate students (AAU 1990). The functions of modern graduate study may thus be said to combine several goals, one of which is regulating the entry of individuals into a field while socializing them into a profession (Merton, Reader, and Kendall 1957; Wiebe 1967).

Graduate education also serves the university by educating research scholars and scientists who, in turn, teach and produce research, often in collaboration with faculty (Hagstrom 1965; Breneman 1970; Snyder 1981). Graduate students also supplement faculty as teachers of undergraduates (see Text Box 1).

---

[1]*Ph.D.* and *doctorate* are used interchangeably throughout this report.

TEXT BOX 1: REQUIREMENTS AND SPECIFIC ASPECTS OF THE DOCTORAL PROGRAM

A doctoral program is an apprenticeship that consists of lecture or laboratory courses, seminars, examinations, discussions, independent study, research, and, in many instances, teaching, designed to help students make significant contributions to knowledge in a reasonable period of time. The first year or two of study is normally a probationary period, during which most of the effort of doctoral students will be devoted to acquiring a working knowledge of the field through study of the literature, taking formal courses and seminars, learning research and experimental techniques, problem-solving, and beginning to teach and do research. After being admitted to candidacy, students devote essentially full time to completing the dissertation research planned with the major adviser, and the dissertation committee. Preparation of the dissertation usually occupies one to three years, depending on the field. An oral defense of the research and dissertation by the candidate before a graduate committee and sometimes other persons invited to attend constitutes the final examination. All requirements for the degree should be available to the student in written form (Council of Graduate Schools 1990, 14).

TRANSFORMATIONS IN SIZE AND ORGANIZATION

In addition to a shift in purpose, graduate education has undergone a dramatic transformation in terms of its size and organization. In 1978 the National Research Council's Board on Human Resource Data and Analyses reported that the number of Ph.D.s awarded in the United States essentially doubled in each decade over the past century. "Quarter-century landmarks show that in 1900 the annual output was about 300; in 1925, about 1,200; in 1950, about 6,000; and in 1974, about 33,000" (NRC 1978). After a period of contraction in the late 1970s and early 1980s, Ph.D. production returned in the late 1980s to those levels recorded in the early 1970s. In the 1990s, degree production has continued to grow (see Figure 1-1). Data from the 1995 Survey of Earned Doctorates revealed that U.S. universities awarded over 41,000 doctorates (NRC 1996).

The transformation that has occurred in graduate education was made possible by a substantial increase in the overall number of institutions offering doctoral programs, especially small programs. The entry of new degree-granting institutions is summarized in Table 1, which shows the proportion of doctoral degrees granted, by year, between 1920 and 1992 in which the awarding institution first granted a Ph.D. As can be seen, most graduates earn their degrees at institutions that first awarded doctorates before 1930. However, since the 1970s the number of doctorates conferred by newer institutions has gradually expanded. Between 1990 and 1992, 8.2 percent of the doctorates conferred were awarded by institutions that recorded the first doctorate after 1970 (NRC 1995a).

The emergence of these newer institutions is also recorded in data from the Carnegie Foundation's *A Classification of Institutions of Higher Education* (1994), which indicate that the number of institutions awarding doctorates grew from 173 in 1970 to 184 in 1976, to 213 in 1987, to 236 in 1994 (see Table 2). Much of the growth occurred in "Doctorate-granting Universities II" whose

TABLE 1-1 Number of Ph.D.s Awarded by U.S. Universities (1920-1992) by Reporting Period and Year in which the Doctorate Records File Recorded the First Ph.D. Awarded by that Institution

Reporting Period		Total	Institution Awarded First Ph.D.							
			Before 1930	In the: 1930s	1940s	1950s	1960s	1970s	1980s	1990-92
1920-29	N	11,935	11,935							
	%	100.0	100.0							
	Annual Average		1,194							
1930-39	N	25,674	25,256	418						
	%	100.0	98.4	1.6						
	Annual Average		2,526	42						
1940-49	N	30,629	28,571	1,850	208					
	%	100.0	93.3	6.0	0.7					
	Annual Average		2,875	185	21					
1950-59	N	80,266	68,601	7,483	3,165	1,017				
	%	100.0	85.5	9.3	3.9	1.3				
	Annual Average		6,860	749	317	102				
1960-69	N	162,071	123,417	15,608	10,711	8,481	3,854			
	%	100.0	76.1	9.6	6.6	5.2	2.4			
	Annual Average		12,342	1,561	1,071	848	385			
1970-79	N	320,936	206,424	30,803	25,537	23,754	26,484	7,934		
	%	100.0	64.3	9.6	8.0	7.4	8.3	2.5		
	Annual Average		20,642	3,080	2,554	2,375	2,648	793		
1980-89	N	319,493	186,283	28,473	27,545	24,275	32,997	18,183	1,737	
	%	100.0	58.3	8.9	8.6	7.6	10.3	5.7	0.5	
	Annual Average		18,628	2,847	2,755	2,428	3,300	1,818	174	
1990-92	N	112,438	62,874	9,597	10,075	8,622	12,140	7,395	1,416	319
	%	100.0	55.9	8.5	9.0	7.7	10.8	6.6	1.3	0.3
	Annual Average		20,958	3,166	3,358	2,877	4,047	2,665	472	106
TOTAL 1920-1992	N	1,063,442	713,361	94,232	77,241	66,149	75,475	33,512	3,153	319
	%	100.0	67.1	8.9	7.3	6.2	7.1	3.2	0.3	<0.1

Notes: Percentages for the reporting period do not total to 100 percent due to rounding. "Annual Average" refers to annual average of the total number of Ph.D.s produced in a period of time.

SOURCE: National Research Council, 1995a.

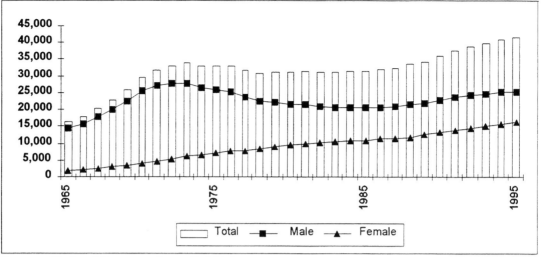

Source: National Research Council, 1996.

FIGURE 1-1 Doctorate recipients, total and by gender, 1965-1995.

TABLE 1-2 Number of Institutions Awarding Doctorates

	1970	1976	1987	1994
Research Universities I	52	51	70	88
Research Universities II	40	47	34	37
Doctorate-Granting I	53	56	51	51
Doctorate-Granting II	28	30	58	60

numbers more than doubled between 1970 and 1994.[2]

As Bowen and Rudenstine observed:

In effect, a new structure has been created. This new structure reflects dramatic increases in the overall number of degree-granting programs, major reductions in the proportion of degrees conferred by highly rated programs, and especially rapid increase in the number of small programs.

From a national point of view, this transformation—in all its dimensions—raises inescapable questions concerning the nature of the system as a whole (p. 56).

[2]Doctorate-granting Universities II are defined by Carnegie as follows: "In addition to offering a full range of baccalaureate programs, the mission of these institutions includes a commitment to graduate education through the doctoral degree. They award annually 20 or more Ph.D. degrees in at least 1 discipline or 10 or more Ph.D. degrees in 3 or more disciplines." See Carnegie Foundation for the Advancement of Teaching (1994) for the full complement of definitions.

CONCERNS ABOUT
RATES OF ATTRITION AND
PATTERNS OF DEGREE ATTAINMENT

From the outset, the "wasteful" consequences of attrition have been a concern of serious educational analysts. One of the few studies of graduate attrition to generate national estimates came from work by Berelson (1960). Berelson's study involved a special-purpose survey of faculty and deans at universities asking them to "estimate the magnitude of attrition" from the cohort of students who had entered graduate school in 1950 (seven years earlier). This "impressionistic" study is one of the few of its type (see Text Box 2). Berelson observed that the attrition rate in graduate school is not high when compared with the undergraduate levels "where it is also about 40 percent. But the matter is perhaps more serious for the graduate school because its selection is supposed to be better; its type of education is much more expensive; and, as with law, its drop-outs stay around longer than the undergraduate drop-outs, half of whom leave in the first year" (Berelson 1960).

Berelson explored the phenomenon of attrition in some detail in his 1960 study. He invited deans, graduate faculty, and recent doctoral degree recipients to give the reasons for attrition at the doctoral level. He states that when he asked the deans and graduate faculty whether it was more a problem of selection or of the programs, they replied in effect that is was "both," but, as Table 3 indicates, "they do not consider [dropping out] the fault of the graduate school. It is either a matter of money or of the student's capability."

TEXT BOX 2: BERELSON'S ACCOUNT OF GRADUATE EDUCATION IN THE UNITED STATES CIRCA 1960

In his seminal work, *Graduate Education in the United States* (1960), Bernard Berelson asks, "Is attrition a major problem of doctoral study, wasting human and institutional resources?" He continues:

> There are certainly those who think so. President [Benjamin] Wright speaks of the 'inordinately high' attrition rate in graduate school and concludes that 'we can save a very considerable number of those who now drop out of graduate school.' While graduate dean at Columbia, Jacques Barzun deplored 'the appalling waste on both sides—of student energy, hope and money, and of faculty time and effort.'

Citing data from questionnaires distributed to graduate deans and graduate faculty members at a number of major research universities, Berelson reports the following estimates from graduate deans: "Of the students who start work toward a doctorate at your institution, about what percentage never finish? Median Institution: 35-40 percent."

When asked, graduate faculty placed attrition at a much lower level—around 20 percent—which Berelson attributes to more "selective attention" on the part of the faculty than the deans who actually maintain the official records.

Berelson admits that 40 percent attrition is high when compared to medical school (at 10 percent) and "the better law schools," but points out that the professional schools typically screen their students more intensively before admission.

Nonetheless, Berelson reports that, "Graduate deans, being closer to the situation administratively, are . . . concerned. Half of them consider [attrition] an important problem for their institutions."

TABLE 1-3 Reasons for Attrition at the Doctoral Level

	Graduate Deans	Graduate Faculty	Recent Recipients
	-------------------------------------percent------------------------------------		
Lack financial resources	69	29	25
Lack intellectual ability to do the work	50	64	52
Lack proper motivation	38	45	47
Lack necessary physical or emotional stamina	33	33	49
Found degree wasn't necessary for what they wanted to do	19	10	12
Disappointed in graduate study and quit	1	12	21

Berelson concludes, however, that the recent recipients are probably "closer to the mark than either the deans or the faculty in their estimates of the disappointment of the doctoral candidates when they leave. . . . The farther from the dean's authority, the more the inclination to blame the graduate school."

Berelson placed graduate attrition somewhere between 20 percent (according to faculty) and 35-40 percent (according to deans). It is important to note, however, that these are impressionistic numbers, based on anecdotal evidence rather than on quantitative analysis, and are likely to be low. Not since Berelson's study have national estimates of attrition from doctoral programs been generated. Instead, analysts turned their attention to a study of factors thought to influence attrition, including lengthy time-to-degree[3] and the social-psychological effects of

changes in the academic environment on student outcome.[4]

ORIGINS AND SCOPE OF THE STUDY

This report responds to a request from the Andrew W. Mellon Foundation for a

and Bae (1990) and Bowen, Lord, and Sosa (1991). Factors that have been shown to be related to long periods of doctoral study include availability of financial support (Abedi and Benkin 1987; Hauptman 1986); excessive teaching responsibilities among graduate students (AAU/AGS 1990); and lack of guidance in the selection and development of a manageable dissertation topic (Council of Graduate Schools 1990, 22).

---

[3]Studies of time-to-degree are numerous but include summary work by Tuckman, Coyle,

[4]Hartnett (1985) notes that until the 1960s very little attention had been given to the academic environment and its impact on students, especially to its role in the decision to drop out.

summary of data sets that could be used to monitor trends in graduate attrition and degree attainment in the sciences and humanities at U.S. universities.[5] The study was conducted under the auspices of the National Research Council's Office of Scientific and Engineering Personnel (OSEP), which invited two members of the OSEP Advisory Committee on Studies and Analyses to serve as an ad hoc panel to oversee the project.

The ad hoc panel began its study with a review of systematic information about graduate attrition and degree attainment in the sciences and humanities. The panel commissioned summaries of known national data bases that have been or could be used to analyze patterns of graduate attrition and degree attainment. These are listed in Appendix A. In addition, the panel commissioned two papers to identify and summarize studies published in the past decade that treated the subject of attrition and degree completion. The results of that review are included in the Annotated Bibliography. The commissioned reviews revealed that there is a distinct and growing body of knowledge about patterns of student departure from doctoral programs in the sciences and humanities. However, most estimates of the degree of graduate attrition have been limited to special purpose studies developed to meet institutional demands for information.

Finally, the panel briefly considered the feasibility of coordinating current efforts to collect information about graduate attrition and degree attainment in order to generate national estimates. There is no question that national data would be desirable, if possible.

Reliable estimates of graduate attrition are in the national interest because of their potential to reduce the waste inherent in the premature departure of talented individuals from advanced preparation in the sciences and humanities, but they did not find such an effort to be feasible within the country's existing diverse system of graduate education. The panel did consider what would be needed for individual institutions to establish their own longitudinal tracking systems, including a list of relevant data elements. These are presented in Appendix B.

ORGANIZATION OF THIS REPORT

This report analyzes the data sources currently available on student attrition from doctoral programs in U.S. universities. Chapter 2 reviews studies that have been conducted in the last few years regarding patterns of attrition and degree attainment. These are studies that have generated precise estimates of attrition from doctoral programs in selected fields at the university level. Many of these studies involve the analysis of university records that also contribute to our growing understanding of when students are likely to "drop out." A second type of study, reviewed in Chapter 3, involves special purpose surveys and analyses that reveal why students leave, pointing to certain features of the academic environment that contribute to the decision to suspend pursuit of the doctorate. Chapter 4 briefly discusses the viability of generating national estimates of graduate attrition and provides conclusions.

---

[5]The sciences are meant here to include the biological sciences, mathematics and the physical sciences, and the social and behavioral sciences. The humanities include such fields as English, history, religion, and modern languages.

REFERENCES

Abedi, Jamal, and Ellen Benkin
1987 "The Effects of Students' Academic, Financial, and Demographic Variables on Time to the Doctorate." *Research in Higher Education* 27 (March 14): 3-14.

Association of American Universities (AAU)
1990 "Institutional Policies to Improve Doctoral Education." A Policy Statement of the Association of American Universities and the Association of Graduate Schools in the AAU. Washington, DC: AAU.

Association of American Universities/ Association of Graduate Schools Project for Research on Doctoral Education (AAU/AGS)
1993 "Participation in Doctoral Education at Major Research Universities by U.S. Citizens, Women and Underrepresented Minorities." *Program Profiles* 1 (April).

Berelson, Bernard
1960 *Graduate Education in the United States.* New York: McGraw Hill.

Bowen, William G., G. Lord, and J.A. Sosa
1991 "Measuring Time to the Doctorate." *Proceedings of the National Academy of Sciences* 88 (3): 713-17.

Bowen, William G., and Neil L. Rudenstine
1992 *In Pursuit of the PhD.* Princeton, NJ: Princeton University Press.

Breneman, David W.
1970 "The Ph.D. Production Process: A Study of Departmental Behavior." Ph.D. diss., University of California, Berkeley.

Carnegie Foundation for the Advancement of Teaching
1994 *A Classification of Institutions of Higher Education.* Princeton, NJ: Princeton University Press.

Council of Graduate Schools (CGS)
1990 *The Doctor of Philosophy Degree: A Policy Statement.* Washington, DC: CGS.

Government-University-Industry Research Roundtable (GUIRR)
1992 *Fateful Choices. The Future of the U.S. Academic Research Enterprise. A Discussion Paper.* Washington, DC: National Academy Press.

Hagstrom, Warren O.
1965 *The Scientific Community.* New York: Basic Books.

Hartnett, Rodney T.
1985 "Trends in Student Quality in Doctoral and Professional Education." *Project on Trends in Academic Talent* (March).

Hauptman, Arthur M.
1986 *Students in Graduate and Professional Education: What We Know and Need to Know.* Washington, DC: AAU.

Merton, R., G. Reader, and P. Kendall
1957 *The Student Physician.* Cambridge, MA: Harvard University Press.

National Research Council (NRC), Board on Human Resource Data and Analyses
1978 *A century of doctorates : data analyses of growth and change : U.S. PhD's—their numbers, origins, characteristics, and the institutions from which they come : a report to the NSF, NEH, and U.S. Office of Education.* Washington, DC: National Academy of Science.

National Research Council (NRC)
1995a *Research-Doctorate Programs in the United States. Continuity and Change.* Washington, DC: National Academy Press.

1995b *Summary Report 1994. Doctorate Recipients from United States Universities.* Washington, DC: National Academy Press.

1996 *1995 Summary Report, Preliminary Tables.* Washington, DC: NRC.

Rudolph, Frederick
1962 *The University: The Autonomy of Academe.* New York: McGraw-Hill.

Snyder, Robert G.
1981 "Federal Support of Graduate Education in the National Sciences: An Inquiry into the Social Impact of Public Policy." Ph.D. diss., Syracuse University.

Tuckman, Howard P., Susan Coyle, and Yupin Bae
1989 "The Lengthening of Time to Completion of the Doctorate Degree." *Research in Higher Education* 30: 503-16.

Veysey, Laurence
1970 *The Emergence of the American University.* Chicago: University of Chicago Press.

Wiebe, R.H.
1967 *The Search for Order, 1877-1970.* New York: Hill and Wang.

2

CURRENT APPROACHES TO THE MEASUREMENT OF GRADUATE ATTRITION

The demand for accurate statistics about graduate attrition arises chiefly from the planning activities of research universities. A number of independent estimates have been generated to meet institutional needs for information. The cumulative effect of studies with different reference dates, different coverage, and different definitions has been to create data sets that generate incompatible statistical results (Duncan 1977).

Despite the limitations, recent studies of student attrition provide a useful basis for understanding the issues and developing future studies of graduate attrition. They do so by suggesting what to measure, how to measure it, and how to interpret results. The sections that follow summarize what is known about graduate attrition from available studies and surveys, beginning with a brief consideration of the concept of attrition itself.

THE CONCEPT OF "ATTRITION" AT THE GRADUATE LEVEL

Education has traditionally proceeded at a predictable tempo in the United States, with students completing their high school (or secondary) education around 18 years of age and their baccalaureate (or tertiary) education five or six years later. The regularity of this pattern is broken, however, when doctoral education is examined. The age at which an individual will earn a Ph.D. or its equivalent varies widely, determined in part by the discipline of study[6] and a number of other factors (see, for example, Tuckman, Coyle, and Bae 1990; Cheney 1988). For example, many graduate students have dependents or outside employment which may directly affect the time it takes to earn a doctorate. Whatever the reason, we do know that the time taken to complete a doctoral degree is considerably longer than the traditional period of four to five years.

Among 1994 doctoral recipients in the sciences and humanities, for example, the median number of years between receipt of the baccalaureate degree and receipt of the Ph.D. ("total time-to-degree") ranged from 8.5 years in the physical sciences to 12.0 years in the humanities (NRC 1995b) (see Figure 2-1). Clearly, some of this time may be accounted for by work or other activities before entering

---

[6]The median age of an individual who earned a doctorate in 1994 varied from 30.0 years for chemists, to 31.2 years for mathematicians, to 36.8 years for anthropologists and sociologists (combined), to 35.2 years for English language and literature majors (NRC 1995a).

14

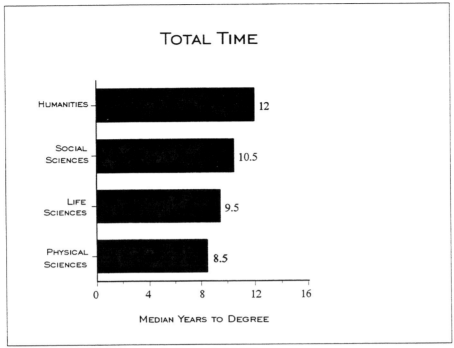

SOURCE: National Research Council, 1995b.

FIGURE 2-1 Median years to doctorate from baccalaureate award, by broad field, 1994.

graduate school, but that pattern is less common in the sciences and humanities than in engineering, education, and other professional areas.

Once enrolled, the median time actually registered in graduate study ("registered time-to-degree") for 1994 graduates ranged from 6.7 years in the physical sciences to 8.5 years in the humanities (see Figure 2-2). This measure is not the same as years enrolled in a doctoral program, since students may enroll first in a master's or other postbaccalaureate program or may take time out for employment once enrolled. Although a longer time-to-degree (registered or not) does not necessarily lead to noncompletion for

any individual student, the likelihood of not completing the degree increases with each additional year in doctoral study, based simply on the fact that each additional year of doctoral study carries with it a positive chance that a student will decide to drop out.

Attrition from graduate study refers to a reduction in the number of individuals pursuing the Ph.D. The most accurate calculation of "attrition" depends on the specification of a group or cohort of students who begin doctoral study at the same time and then a later look at that cohort to determine the proportion of students having completed their degrees by a certain time (to derive a "completion rate") or the proportion of

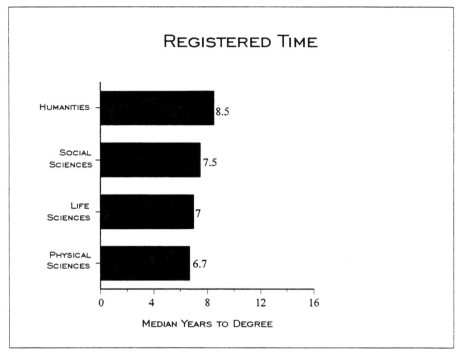

SOURCE: National Research Council, 1995b.

FIGURE 2-2 Median years to doctorate from first registration, by broad field, 1994.

students who are no longer enrolled ("attrition rate").[7]

It is difficult to estimate a completion rate for doctoral study for several reasons. First, Ph.D. programs vary widely in their definition of when students begin doctoral study, even within the same university. A review of the literature on higher education suggests that there are essentially three models for pursuing the Ph.D. in the sciences and humanities at U.S. universities. The American Model treats the student who has entered the first post-baccalaureate year of study as a member of the Ph.D. program. The German Model, evident in many U.S. universities, considers an individual as a Ph.D. student only when that individual has been admitted to candidacy. The M.A.-First Model is apparent in certain professional fields such as engineering or education, whereby a student may enter a Ph.D. program only after receipt of the master's degree, with or without intervening work experience. Complicating this picture further are the students who enter a master's program and then switch to the Ph.D., and those who transfer from other graduate degree programs.

---

[7]In addition to students no longer enrolled, there are two other groups of "noncompleters": individuals who are still enrolled in the program and those who have "stopped out." This latter group includes students who are not enrolled at a particular time but may return to the program in the future. Thus, at any given time, attrition equals the original cohort of students minus "completers" minus "those still enrolled" minus those who have "stopped out."

Second, there is no fixed time beyond which students can be considered no longer enrolled in doctoral study. Institutions vary widely in the maximum number of years permitted for students to complete the Ph.D., typically ranging from five to 10 years after entry into doctoral study. Even if graduate schools have a written policy, exceptions for individual students are often made. Many individuals start and stop their graduate study, taking leaves of absence for personal or professional reasons, sometimes returning years later to complete their degrees. The combination of these factors makes it impossible to determine decisively when students should no longer be considered in pursuit of the doctorate. Researchers interested in measuring attrition in the face of these enrollment irregularities have approached the definitional problem in a variety of ways. Most have established an "operational definition" of graduate attrition by setting arbitrary cutoff points for completion and a uniform starting point for entry.

Many researchers use the American model to define the start of doctoral study, assuming that a student's first enrollment in graduate study after the baccalaureate constitutes entry into a doctoral program. Cutoff points for degree completion have been established variously at 6, 10, and sometimes 11 years after entry into graduate programs. The use of a cutoff point such as this has the advantage of treating all "non-enrolled" students as "non-completers" but obviously cannot accurately account for those students who eventually return to the program and complete their degrees (see Text Box 3).

CONTEMPORARY ESTIMATES OF ATTRITION

Studies of graduate attrition and degree attainment can range from theoretical studies that aim to build or test models of student persistence to empirical studies that rely on scientific samples from carefully framed populations. Although restricted to samples involving a single institution or smaller sets of institutions, recent studies have been more rigorously quantitative.[8] A flurry of quantitative studies of attrition appeared in the 1980s, involving analysis of student records or the linkage of data sets from which estimates of attrition could be made. Selected examples of quantitative studies are presented below.

Student records provide a rich data set that plots the career trajectory of the doctoral work force at a critical phase of its unfolding. With the advent of computerized data systems, there has been a small but increasing trend toward the analysis of student records for purposes of estimating graduate attrition. Three sets of studies in particular have achieved national attention for the quality of their analyses: (1) work by Nerad (1991) and Nerad and Cerny (1991) that focuses on graduate attrition at the University of California at Berkeley; (2) a study by Miselis, McManus, and Kraus (1991) that uses data from the University of Pennsylvania; and (3) a comprehensive assessment of graduate

---

[8]Bowen and Rudenstine (1992) report that Tucker and his colleagues at Michigan State University attempted to analyze completion rates at 24 universities as early as 1964 using longitudinal student records in an attempt to give more precision to estimates of graduate attrition. However, they apparently restricted their analyses to students holding a master's degree, thereby removing early attrition from their estimates.

TEXT BOX 3

The most recent notable attempt to generate a common definition of completion rates has been offered by Bowen and Rudenstine (1992):

"The main complication in studying all aspects of the effectiveness of graduate education—and certainly in defining and measuring completion rates—is that students pursue doctorates, on and off, over many years. For a small number of students, pursuit of the PhD becomes almost a lifelong endeavor. Since the percentage of each entering cohort who earn the doctorate rises as the number of years since entry increases, we have elected to work primarily with two kinds of completion rates: minimum completion rates (MCR) and truncated completion rates (TCR).

"Perhaps the easiest way to define these rates is by using a set of hypothetical numbers. Suppose that:

- 100 students enter graduate study in English in 1972;
- By 1978, 50 have earned doctorates, 25 have ceased pursuing the doctorate, and 25 are still enrolled;
- By 1982, 60 have earned the doctorate, 32 have ceased pursuing the doctorate, and 8 are still enrolled.

The minimum completion rate is the percentage of the entering cohort who have earned the doctorate *by a specified year*. In this example, the MCR was 50 percent in 1978 and 60 percent in 1982. Obviously, the MCR rises with the number of years that have elapsed between entry to graduate school and the year in which the measurement is made. Because of its simplicity and wide applicability, this is the completion rate that is used most frequently in this study, and whenever we refer simply to the completion rate (with no modifier), this is the concept that is being used. The MCR can be misleading, however, especially when time series comparisons are being made, and that is why we also use the concept of the truncated completion rate.

"The truncated completion rate is the percentage of an entering cohort who earned the doctorate *within a specified number of years from entry to graduate study*. In this example, the TCR after six years was 50 percent in 1978, as well as in 1982 and all subsequent years, since it is impossible for more students to earn degrees within a time interval once the limit of that interval has been exceeded. If the cutoff number of years had been set at ten rather than at six, the TCR could not have been measured in 1978 and would have been 60 percent in 1982 and all subsequent years. Truncated completion rates are particularly useful when comparisons are being made between outcomes for recent cohorts (who will have had only a limited number of years in which to complete their studies) and outcomes for earlier cohorts.

"A further complication in computing completion rates concerns transfers. The completion rates that we calculate on the basis of the Ten-University data set treat all students who have left each university as having dropped out, even though some may have completed a PhD after transferring to another university. The National Fellowship data set, on the other hand, tracks individual students who have moved from one university to another, and the completion rates including transfers will, of course, be somewhat higher than the corresponding completion rates that do not allow for transfers" (pp. 106-107).

18

education by Bowen and Rudenstine that uses a ten-university data set.[9]

University of California at Berkeley

Maresi Nerad and Joseph Cerny have undertaken a number of special studies of graduate education at the University of California at Berkeley using the institution's administrative files. One study involved the analysis of completion patterns for cohorts who entered in 1978 and 1979 (see Text Box 4). Responding to concerns about anticipated shortages of skilled personnel, the Graduate Division broke from its "traditional role" and undertook research "to design and implement programs that encourage students to complete their degrees and to do so in a reasonable amount of time" (Nerad and Cerny 1991, 1).

The Berkeley study proceeded in five steps. The first step involved developing a number of statistical analyses based on demographic data about the graduate students to determine such things as average time-to-degree and the points in the program at which students tended to leave. Only students who identified themselves as working toward the doctoral degree were included in the study.

The analysis utilized cohorts entering in 1978 and 1979 and looked at completion rates as measured in November 1989 when "most of the students, by then, should have had sufficient time to complete their doctoral programs." As Figure 2-3 indicates (1) 24 percent left during their first three years of study,[10] (2) 10 percent left after advancement to candidacy, (3) 58 percent completed doctoral degrees, and (4) another 8 percent were "pending." Doctoral completion rates varied significantly by field, as illustrated in Figure 2-4. The biological and physical sciences had the highest completion rates while the arts, languages, and literature had the lowest.

The authors note that Berkeley may be fairly typical, "at least among public universities," citing as evidence Benkin's work (1984) at the University of California at Los Angeles (UCLA), which reveals that about 30 percent of UCLA students leave during the early period of doctoral study.

University of Pennsylvania

Concerned for some time that graduate students were taking too long to complete their doctorates, Karen Miselis, William McManus, and Eileen Kraus (1991) undertook a project in the School of Arts and Sciences at the University of Pennsylvania to conduct "a very thorough and informative attrition and time-to-degree study" (see Text Box 5). The authors spent over a year collecting, cleaning, and analyzing a wide variety of academic, demographic, and financial data for each student.

There were several sources of information available in both electronic and paper form. The registrar had student activity tapes back to Fall 1973 and transcripts for all students who ever attended the University. Student Financial Aid had

---

[9]The universities include Berkeley, Chicago, Columbia, Cornell, Harvard, Michigan, Princeton, Stanford, University of North Carolina, and Yale.

---

[10]Most of these students (83 percent) earned a master's degree along the way.

TEXT BOX 4: FROM FACTS TO ACTION

Mounting concern over the "anticipated shortage of college teachers, scientists, and engineers" led Maresi Nerad and Joseph Cerny (1991) to analyze completion rates for students entering in 1978 and 1979, as measured in November 1989, and attrition patterns from Ph.D. programs at the University of California at Berkeley. Fifty-eight percent had completed doctoral degrees, with 72 percent doing so in the biological sciences, 69 percent in the physical sciences, 39 percent in the arts, and 37 percent in the languages and literature (the lowest).

In addition, the authors arranged for the administrators in the Graduate Division to meet monthly with representatives of the Graduate Council to specify recommendations for action, such as "a new policy requiring students to meet annually with at least two members of their dissertation committee to review their progress on their dissertations and to map out a plan for the following year."

Contrary to popular belief, the majority of graduate students who did not earn their doctorates left the program before advancement to candidacy for the Ph.D., not after. Through in-depth interviews, the authors asked 40 UC-Berkeley students from history, English, French, and sociology why they left doctoral studies. These students' answers were compared with students from psychology and biochemistry who had just completed their dissertations and who were asked how they moved from one stage of doctoral work to the next stage. Six similar patterns were found for students who had left doctoral studies in the humanities and social sciences:

1. Students in departments that require a M.A. thesis spent an excessive amount of time polishing the thesis.

2. Humanities and social science students over prepared for their orals.

3. After having passed the qualifying exam, these students spent between one and two years searching for a dissertation topic and writing a dissertation prospectus.

4. Humanities and social science students wrote their dissertations in total isolation.

5. These students perceived the course work, orals, and prospectus-writing stages of their doctoral programs as *hurdles* that needed to be jumped, but not as steps leading to the completion of their dissertations.

6. Many humanities and social science students complained that the department and faculty failed to assist them in preparing for orals, in applying for grants, and in the actual writing of their dissertations.

Finally, Nerad and Cerny "developed recommendations and designed and implemented activities" to work to decrease time-to-degree and lower attrition:

Faculty. The Graduate Division initiated a monthly seminar involving faculty, department chairs, deans, and graduate students to "inform and sensitize a part of the campus community, particularly the faculty, about these particular issues of graduate education."

Graduate Students. Meetings were initiated with interdepartmental student focus groups. Besides functioning as a "support group" for students, the focus groups gave students a chance to share problems and to understand what other departments were doing for their students. In addition, "the Graduate Division developed a better understanding about the specific needs of students" and gathered useful ideas for educational activities to meet their needs.

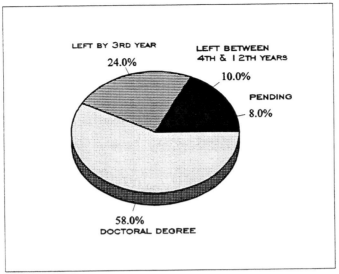

LEFT BY 3RD YEAR
24.0%

LEFT BETWEEN
4TH & 12TH YEARS
10.0%

PENDING
8.0%

58.0%
DOCTORAL DEGREE

SOURCE: Nerad and Cerny, 1991.

FIGURE 2-3 University of California at Berkeley progression status of 1978-79 cohorts, as of November 1989.

tapes going back to 1979, and Personnel/ Payroll tapes were available back to 1974.

The authors found that one of the factors making the study of graduate programs more difficult than studies of undergraduate programs is the fact that there is not "one" doctoral program, but "many": "Every Ph.D.-granting department can set its own policies and is quite distinct in its program from others within the University."

Findings are presented in Figure 2-5 for three divisions at the University of Pennsylvania: the humanities, the social sciences, and the natural sciences. The authors observe major differences among divisions with regard to attrition:

The Natural Sciences tend to lose their students early, while other divisions continue to lose students even after a decade of study. For instance, the Humanities department with the worst record on attrition after 6 years had lost 54 percent. After 10 years of study, that department had lost another 25 percent, to have a cumulative attrition rate of 79 percent. Within the Natural Sciences, however, the cumulative attrition rates at 6 years post-matriculation and 10 years post-matriculation are virtually identical.

The study further noted that the humanities have consistently graduated less than 50 percent of their matriculants. For the natural sciences, from 60 to 75 percent typically finish successfully, while the social sciences reveal a range of graduation rates from 33 to 54 percent over a 10-year period.

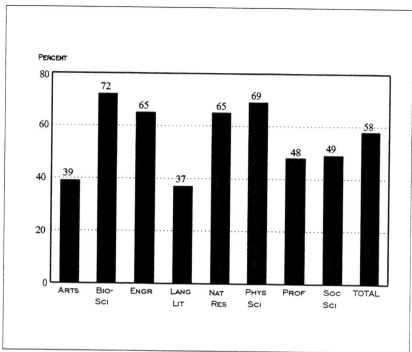

SOURCE: Nerad and Cerny, 1991.

FIGURE 2-4 Doctoral completion rates for the 1978-79 cohort at the University of California at Berkeley, by field and gender, November 1989.

The Ten-University Data Set

In 1989 William Bowen and Neil Rudenstine undertook a project to "[p]lace doctoral programs in the arts and sciences within the larger context of doctoral education in all fields and examine trends in recipients of Ph.D.s over the last 35 years . . ." (Bowen and Rudenstine 1992, 8). The authors were interested in knowing, among other things, how the overall "system" of graduate education has been affected by the expansion of the 1960s and subsequent contraction in enrollments and degrees conferred.

Noting that graduate education has many outcomes, Bowen and Rudenstine focus attention on completion rates and time-to-degree using data from a set of 10 institutions for entering cohorts in six specific fields: English, history, economics, political science, mathematics, and physics. The authors acknowledge that distinguishing Ph.D. candidates from students who entered graduate school only to earn a master's degree was "a particularly vexing problem." The solution was to ask the universities to send records only for those entering students who were regarded at the time of entry as interested in obtaining a Ph.D., even though it was understood that in certain programs students would formally become Ph.D. candidates only after completing certain requirements.

TEXT BOX 5: ANALYSIS OF PH.D. STUDENT ATTRITION AT THE UNIVERSITY OF PENNSYLVANIA

In 1991 Karen Miselis, William McManus, and Eileen Kraus presented a paper describing their experience in "collecting, cleaning, and analyzing data" about attrition and time-to-degree. The authors spent over a year on the project using data from five of the 36 separate graduate groups in the School of Arts and Sciences at the University of Pennsylvania. They gathered a wide variety of academic, demographic, and financial data for each student in order to "build the data base of graduate student information required for this study."

Miselis and her colleagues described numerous issues involved in creating the computerized data system, noting two general problems they encountered:

The first had to do with errors in the data, and the second with student characteristics. In addition to errors associated with miss-keying data and data

redundancy, we encountered data errors that resulted from the way the data were created. Establishing the degree sought, Ph.D. or M.A., was extremely important and yet difficult to do.

Our biggest data problem was with the financial aid data. The financial aid tapes supplied us with information on fellowship, teaching assistantship, and won support for 1979 through 1989 only and the tape for 1985 had been lost. The payroll tape supplied us with information on grant support for Fall 1974 through Spring 1989 but contained no information on loans. We decided not to use any of the financial aid data because of the analytic problems induced by the missing year's worth of data and because the breadth of the data was so short compared to payroll.

The paper describes the final data set, findings, and proposed institutional reforms. Above all, the study demonstrates the feasibility and utility of creating institutional data sets that address graduate attrition and degree completion.

Fortunately, this problem of distinguishing M.A.-only candidates from likely Ph.D. candidates did not exist in the majority of programs included in this study, since most of these programs either admit only Ph.D. candidates or distinguish at admission those on the M.A. track from those on the Ph.D. track. Some ambiguities were never resolved satisfactorily, but most universities that had this problem seem to have been successful in segregating the records of those entering students who were interested from the beginning in obtaining the Ph.D. (p. 291).

From this data set, Bowen and Rudenstine provide many types of analyses.

In the area of "outcomes" they provide information about patterns of attrition from graduate study. As Figure 2-6 illustrates, the authors were able to calculate the stages at which individuals left graduate study at these 10 universities: (1) before starting the second year of study; (2) after starting the second year, but before completing all requirements for the Ph.D. other than the dissertation; and (3) after completing all requirements but the dissertation (ABD). For the 1972-1976 entering cohort, the probability of achieving second-year status was 87 percent; the probability of achieving ABD status given second-year status was about 80 percent; and the probability of achieving the Ph.D. given ABD status was 81 percent.

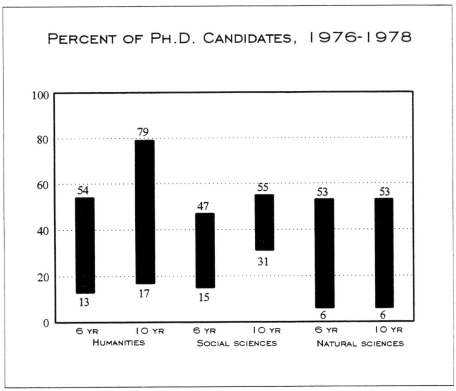

SOURCE: Miselis, McManus, and Krause, 1991.

FIGURE 2-5 Attrition patterns for the 1976-1978 cohort in three divisions at the University of Pennsylvania, high and low departments, after 6 and 10 years.

The authors also report differences in attrition by major field, which are summarized in Figure 2-7. They note that the conditional probability of completing a dissertation in mathematics or physics once a student has achieved ABD status was about 90 percent for the two cohorts that were analyzed. Among English, history, and political science students the corresponding conditional probability was 79 percent for the 1967-1971 cohort and just 75 percent for the 1972-1976 cohort. Several explanations are offered for the differences across fields. Financial support continues to be an important factor in degree completion, and there is more support available in the natural sciences than in the humanities or social sciences and less reliance on teaching assistantships. However, even when financial support was not an issue (in the case of fellowship recipients), differences in completion rates persisted. Bowen and Rudenstine assert that the structure of the graduate programs themselves plays a large role in completion. Programs in the physical sciences are more structured, setting out more uniform degree requirements and providing closer faculty supervision. Programs in the humanities are usually less structured, providing multiple options for completing requirements and more independent study. At the dissertation level especially, students in the physical sciences doing their research in a laboratory have ready access to faculty help, are monitored, and interact regularly with

24

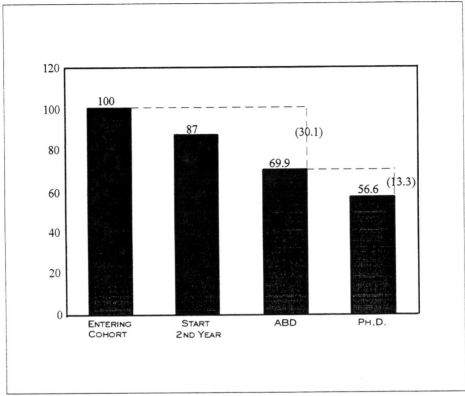

Note: Data report "percent" of each entering cohort.

SOURCE: Bowen and Rudenstine, 1992.

FIGURE 2-6 Attrition by stage, six-field total, 1972-1976 entering cohorts.

colleagues. Students in the humanities doing independent library research have to seek out faculty help, may not receive regular monitoring, and may work alone for long periods of time.

Other Institutions

A number of other studies provide us with some estimates of attrition, if only as a by-product of other analyses. These studies include work by Bodian at the University of Maryland (1987), Dolph at Georgia State (1983), Valentine at West Virginia University (1987), Zwick and Brown using data from Northwestern University (1990), and Ehrenberg and Mavros at Cornell (1992).

Administrative records and statistical data sets thus offer an opportunity to monitor trends in attrition. They do not alone provide explanatory power often sought by educational planners and policy makers. More theoretically grounded studies are needed to probe relationships among variables (Bradburn and Gilford 1990), some of which are described in the next section.

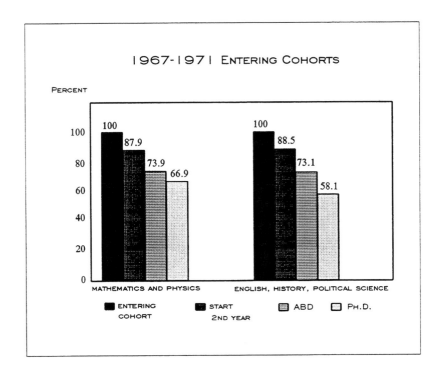

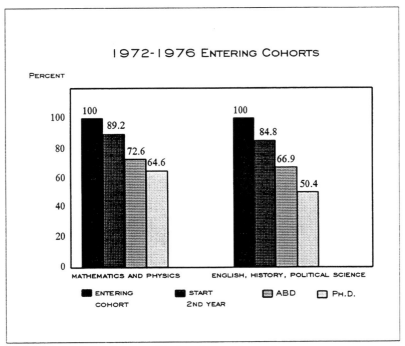

Note: Data report "percent" of each entering cohort.

SOURCE: Bowen and Rudenstine, 1992.

FIGURE 2-7 Attrition by stage and fields, 1967-1971 and 1972-1976 entering cohorts.

26

REFERENCES

Benkin, Ellen M.
1984 "Where Have All the Doctoral Students Gone? A Study of Doctoral Students' Attrition at UCLA." Ph.D. diss., University of California, Los Angeles.

Bodian, Lester Hal
1987 "Career Instrumentality of Degree Completion as a Factor in Doctoral Student Attrition." Ph.D. diss., University of Maryland.

Bowen, William G., and Neil L. Rudenstine
1992 *In Pursuit of the PhD.* Princeton, NJ: Princeton University Press.

Bradburn, N.M., and D. Gilford
1990 *A Framework and Principles for International Comparative Studies in Education.* Washington, DC: National Academy Press.

Cheney, Lynne V.
1988 *Humanities in America.* Washington, DC: National Endowment for the Humanities.

Dolph, Robert F.
1983 "Factors Relating to Success or Failure in Obtaining the Doctorate." Ph.D. diss., Georgia State University.

Duncan, Joseph W.
1977 "Priority Setting in the Coming Decade." *Statistical Reporter Series,* No. 77-7. Washington, DC: Office of Management and Budget.

Ehrenberg, R.G., and Mavros, P.G.
1995 "Do Doctoral Students' Financial Support Patterns Affect Their Times-To-Degree and Completion Probabilities?" *Journal of Human Resources* 30 (3): 581-609.

Miselis, Karen L., William McManus, and Eileen Kraus
1991 "We Can Improve Our Graduate Programs: Analysis of Ph.D. Student Attrition and Time-to-Degree at the University of Pennsylvania." Paper presented at the Annual Forum of the Association of Institutional Research, San Francisco, California, May 29.

National Research Council (NRC)
1995a *Summary Report 1994. Doctorate Recipients from United States Universities.* Washington, DC: National Academy Press.

1995b *1994 Survey of Earned Doctorates, Special Tabulations.* Washington, DC: NRC.

Nerad, Maresi
1991 *Doctoral Education at the University of California and Factors Affecting Time-To-Degree.* Oakland, CA: Office of the President, University of California.

Nerad, Maresi, and Joseph Cerny
1991 "From Facts to Action: Expanding the Educational Role of the Graduate Division." *Communicator* (May Special Edition). Washington, D.C.: Council of Graduate Schools.

Tuckman, Howard P., Susan Coyle, and Yupin Bae
1989 "The Lengthening of Time to Completion of the Doctorate Degree." *Research in Higher Education* 30: 503-16.

Valentine, Nancy L.
1987 "Factors Related to Attrition from Doctor of Education Programs." Paper presented at annual meeting of the Association of Institutional Research, Kansas City, Missouri, May 3-6.

Zwick, Rebecca, and Henry I. Braun
1988 *Methods for Analyzing the Attainment of Graduate School Milestones: A Case Study.* GRE Board Professional Report No. 86-3P. Princeton, NJ: Educational Testing Service.

3

IDENTIFYING FACTORS THOUGHT
TO CONTRIBUTE TO GRADUATE ATTRITION

INTERVIEWS
WITH NONCOMPLETERS

Qualitative studies have been conducted in conjunction with more formal survey work, or they may be carried out strictly in the form of case studies used initially to document relationships of interest to the investigator. Studies of attrition—whether at the graduate or undergraduate level—have frequently involved analyses of variables thought to be related to attrition. These studies often involve interviews with former students either as they exit a graduate program (Nerad and Cerny 1991) or after they have entered the workforce (Jacks et al. 1983; Arnold, Mares, and Calkins 1986; Valentine 1987) (see Text Box 6).

LONGITUDINAL ANALYSES
OF LINKED DATA SETS

A quantitative approach used with some degree of success is the analysis of degree completion patterns derived from longitudinal analyses of linked data sets. In this method, records for students in one data set may be linked with information in another data set to examine the role of "antecedent conditions" that account for differences in completion outcomes.

The methodological difficulties encountered in linking separate data sets maintained by different organizations for the purposes of longitudinal analysis are demonstrated by the paucity of studies of this kind.[11] Nonetheless, this technique has significant potential for understanding, in a systematic way, factors contributing to attrition over time.

---

[11]There are obviously many problems encountered with this procedure, some of which arise from the fact that different files are maintained for different purposes and may not collect the information directly of interest to the researcher. In addition, strict legal restraints and confidentiality rulings appropriately determine which data sets are available for research purposes. Tanur (1982) believes that "as information demands become greater, it is natural to look for sources of data that involve less burden on respondents and lower collection costs than those incurred by surveys or experiments."

TEXT BOX 6: THE ABCs OF ABDs

In 1983 Penelope Jacks and her colleagues at the Georgia Institute of Technology published a "narrative portrait" of 25 individuals who had completed all doctoral degree requirements except the dissertation ("all but dissertation" or ABD). Most had attended graduate school in the late 1960s, and most of those interviewed were men. Interviews were conducted by telephone with questions focused on three major issues:

· reasons for leaving the doctoral program
· possible impacts on life and career of being "ABD"
· perceived value of the Ph.D.

The project was conducted in conjunction with a larger survey of Ph.D.s in six fields (psychology, sociology, zoology, electrical engineering, and biochemistry) that focused on the graduate school experiences and career outcomes of scientists who actually completed their doctoral degrees around 1970 (see Porter et al. 1981).

After "financial difficulties," the most frequently cited reason for leaving doctoral programs revolved around problems with advisors or doctoral committees. Some respondents reported that advisors were inaccessible owing to research work and/or travel schedules, or that dissertation committees lacked interest in a student's project. In other words, there was no one there "to encourage and give good ideas" to the students. The authors also reported that no one gave only one reason for not completing the dissertation:

Often people began the interview by giving a single 'stock' explanation, but as the interview progressed several issues emerged, and the first one mentioned was not necessarily the most significant. A few respondents admitted that they had never before given a great deal of thought to the experience as a whole.

The authors concluded that formal doctoral preparation may be only as effective as "the informal support system that faculty and peers provide, and in some programs, for some people, such support is never provided."

Issues in Measurement

The work by Jacks and her colleagues is by no means a rigorous statistical account of attrition from doctoral programs. As the authors suggest, the study may best be considered "a collective biography of would-be scientists who consented to reflect in 1980 on their experiences in graduate school."

As a measurement tool, prosopography (development of the collective biography) offers the potential for augmenting statistical profiles of patterns of attrition by revealing the factors which lay behind the observed behavior.

EDUCATIONAL TESTING SERVICE

A study of Ph.D. degree completion involving the linking of data sets was conducted by Rebecca Zwick at the Educational Testing Service (ETS) in 1991 (see Text Box 7). Zwick investigated the graduate careers of nearly 5,000 Ph.D.-seeking students from 11 departments in each of three major research universities. She initially invited 20 universities to determine "whether they maintained data bases that would lend themselves to the planned analyses and whether they would be willing to participate in the study." The key requirement was that information was needed at the

TEXT BOX 7:
PATTERNS OF ATTAINMENT OF PH.D.
CANDIDACY AND DEGREE COMPLETION

In 1991 Rebecca Zwick presented an analysis of graduate school careers at three universities that examined attainment patterns of 5,000 Ph.D. students in 11 departments during the years 1978 through 1985. One goal of the study was to determine how patterns of Ph.D. attainment varied across and within the institutions. Another goal was to determine the extent to which scores on the Graduate Record Examination (GRE) and undergraduate grade point average (UGPA) predicted observed differences.

A general finding was that candidacy and graduation rates in the eight years following matriculation were higher in "quantitatively oriented departments"—chemistry, physics, mathematics, and computer science—than in the humanities and social sciences. Chemistry generally showed the highest candidacy rates, while English and philosophy showed the lowest. Graduation rates revealed a similar pattern.

A correlational analysis explored the association of candidacy and graduation with the GRE verbal score, the GRE quantitative score, and the UGPA. The analysis indicated that GRE scores and the UGPA were almost entirely unrelated to the achievement of candidacy and graduation. Arguing that these graduate school matriculants had already been selected on the basis of those scores, Zwick suggests: "Within the select population of graduate students, it is likely that such personality factors as perseverance . . . play a crucial role in determining whether candidacy and graduation are achieved."

individual student level for at least five consecutive years of enrollment. Variables of interest to Zwick included entry date, department, citizenship, ethnicity (at least for U.S. citizens), gender, undergraduate grade point average, scores on the Graduate Record Exam (GRE), date of advancement to candidacy, and date of graduation. A further requirement was that the data be in machine-readable form. As one might imagine, attrition among the participating institutions themselves was large:

Six of the twenty schools that were contacted initially agreed to participate. In most cases, refusals were due to the unavailability of the required data. It was subsequently determined that two of the original six participating schools could not supply data on the variables of interest. A third school withdrew because no staff were available to create the needed data tapes. This left three participating schools, all of which are large research universities (Zwick 1991).

Zwick notes that for the years prior to 1982, the data base from School 1 did not include GRE scores. Therefore, with the university's permission, records from School 1 were linked to the GRE data base at ETS to obtain the scores for students in the departments selected for study. In the end, the percentage of students for whom GRE scores were available ranged from 75 to 100 percent across the 11 departments at the three schools.

The author analyzed undergraduate grade point average (UGPA) and GRE quantitative (GREQ) and GRE verbal (GREV) scores relative to admission to candidacy and graduation. Zwick reports that, in general, the prediction was "very poor," with median correlations ranging from -.09 to .11. "UGPA and GREQ were somewhat more likely to be positively related to candidacy and graduation than was GREV." Variations across departments in the size of the correlation did not appear to follow any consistent pattern. Nevertheless, "the results do not imply that the GRE and UGPA were useless as admissions criteria" since those who were not admitted were not observed.

These studies demonstrate the utility of linking data sets in examinations of completion patterns. More formal analysis of these variables and other antecedent conditions might be considered by the research community as the opportunity to conduct this type of analysis presents itself again.

REFERENCES

Arnold, Louise, Kenneth R. Mares, and E. Virginia Calkins
1986   "Exit Interviews Reveal Why Students Leave a BA-MD Degree Program Prematurely." *College and University* 62: 34-47.

Jacks, Penelope, Daryl E. Chubin, Alan L. Porter, and Terry Connolly
1983   "The ABCs of ABDs: A Study of Incomplete Doctorates." *Improving College and University Teaching* 31: 74-81.

Nerad, Maresi, and Joseph Cerny
1991   "From Facts to Action: Expanding the Educational Role of the Graduate Division." *Communicator* (May Special Edition). Washington, DC: Council of Graduate Schools.

Porter, A., D. Chubin, M. Boeckmann, T. Connolly, and P. Rossi
1981   "A Cross-Disciplinary Assessment of the Role of the Doctoral Dissertation in Career Productivity." Report to the National Science Foundation, Division of Science Resources Studies. Atlanta, GA: School of Industrial and Systems Engineering, Georgia Institute of Technology.

Tanur, Judith
1982   "Advances in Methods for Large-Scale Surveys and Experiments." In *Behavioral and Social Research: A National Resource, Part II*, edited by R. Adams, N. Smelser, and D. Treimon. Washington, DC: National Academy Press.

Valentine, Nancy L.
1987   "Factors Related to Attrition from Doctor of Education Programs." Paper presented at annual meeting of the Association of Institutional Research, Kansas City, Missouri, May 3-6.

Zwick, Rebecca
1991   *An Analysis of Graduate School Careers in Three Universities: Differences in Attainment Patterns Across Academic Programs and Demographic Groups.* Princeton, NJ: Educational Testing Service.

4

CONCLUSION

Our confidence in the effectiveness of graduate education in the United States depends, to a large extent, on the statistics that describe the outcomes of the enterprise. Accurate and reliable statistics that document enrollment patterns, degrees conferred, attrition rates, and postgraduate plans are vital to educators and policy makers for monitoring the performance of the system. They are also useful to prospective graduate students in making choices about where and whether to enroll.

Any system designed to produce national estimates of graduate attrition at U.S. universities would require the integration or linking of diverse data collection efforts. Such an integrated data set would need to involve a comprehensive system of statistics generated by a sample of institutions drawn from the full range of universities offering doctoral preparation. The information that is gathered would document critical aspects of student progress through post-baccalaureate studies to permit the development of policies to reduce attrition and increase degree completion.

Given the decentralized nature of graduate education in this country, however, the ability to collect and report national estimates of attrition is questionable. To a large extent, systematic information about graduate education in this country is a by-product of the statistical activities of many independent programs. Data collection is carried out by educational institutions, professional societies, state and federal agencies, and private foundations. Some data are collected in cooperation with federal laws that require statistics to monitor compliance of the higher education community with relevant civil rights statutes, but most statistics about graduate education are generated to meet short-term institutional needs for specific information, and definitions vary to meet each individual context and information needs.

Even if there were a mechanism to collect and analyze national data on graduate attrition, the absence of comparability among the data would make systematic analysis very difficult for a number of reasons. First, the locus of data collection would necessarily be the individual university since that is the only place where individual student records are kept. Any national estimates would depend on the use of institutional administrative records (which vary markedly in content), the degree of automation, and the care with which they are maintained.

Second, because each institution maintains its own records, definitions of key variables would differ significantly from one university to the next. The critical definitions of when doctoral education begins and when students are considered to have "left" the program are set by each institution and, in some cases, by each separate graduate program.

Third, even if data could be collected or compiled using common definitions, the diverse structure of graduate programs would make comparison difficult. Rates of attrition would be meaningful only in the context of a particular program's admissions policies (open or selective) and its willingness to permit students to reenter who have dropped out. For example, less selective programs might expect higher rates of attrition, while programs with lenient reentry rules might have lower rates of attrition but longer time-to-degree.

A case in point is the Association of American Universities (AAU)/Association of Graduate Schools (AGS) Project for Research on Doctoral Education. With longitudinal data on individual students from 1989 to the present, this project has the potential to yield systematic, ongoing information on graduate student attrition, at least at major research universities. It is constrained, however, by many of the difficulties of comparability and definition discussed here (see Text Box 8).

In the face of such variability across programs, the panel concludes that it is not feasible or cost effective to attempt to coordinate current efforts to collect information about graduate attrition and degree attainment in order to generate national estimates.

Having said that, we encourage individual institutions and researchers to continue studies of graduate attrition. Such studies can provide valuable insight to institutions so that students who leave do so by design and not through inattention.

TEXT BOX 8: THE AAU/AGS PROJECT FOR RESEARCH ON DOCTORAL EDUCATION

Hosted by the Educational Testing Service, the AAU/AGS Project for Research on Doctoral Education collects and maintains longitudinal data on individual students in Ph.D. programs in ten selected fields at approximately forty research universities (see Appendix A for details). The project has many of the features that would be required of a national, systematic effort to study graduate student attrition: it is national in scope; it includes a range of science and humanities fields; it collects from institutions data on individual graduate students; and it maintains a longitudinal data base of changes in students' degree status over time. Data are available from the fall of 1989.

One of the most difficult challenges in data analysis, as reported by project staff, is the variability in definitions of graduate student enrollment and degree status. The institutions participating in the project, and even departments within the same institution, define student status differently. They also may impose different re-quirements for the time limit allowed for degree completion, the need for students to be registered continuously, and the procedures for reentering after having "stopped out."

In this data base, students in a degree program who have not graduated and not officially left the program are divided into "active" and "inactive" students. Inactive students are defined as those who are not enrolled but are eligible to enroll, as far as is known by the institution. Inactive students may or may not be making progress toward their degrees; they may be studying for examinations or writing their dissertation; they may have left the program without informing anyone; or they may have taken a temporary break. The ambiguity of the status of "inactive" students makes it difficult to determine an exact number of students to include in calculating attrition.

Over time, of course, most students in a given cohort will have completed their degree requirements or left the program. In the meantime, though, researchers wanting to use these data to study attrition will have to establish their own method to categorize the various types of inactive students.

ANNOTATED BIBLIOGRAPHY

This bibliography has been designed to provide interested individuals with a list of recent readings relevant to the analysis of graduate attrition in the sciences and humanities. The bibliography is not intended to serve as a comprehensive list of publications in this area; rather it is meant to serve as a mechanism to orient readers to literature on this topic.

Abedi, Jamal, and Ellen Benkin
1987 "The Effects of Students' Academic, Financial, and Demographic Variables on Time to the Doctorate." *Research in Higher Education* 27 (March 14): 3-14.

The most important variable in time-to-degree was the source of support during graduate school. "Own earnings" especially add to time-to-degree. Fifth in importance was field of study. Also included are data from the National Research Council's Doctorates Records File on 4,255 students receiving doctoral degrees at UCLA between 1976 and 1985.

Arnold, Louise, Kenneth R. Mares, and E. Virginia Calkins
1986 "Exit Interviews Reveal Why Students Leave a BA-MD Degree Program Prematurely." *College and University* 62: 34-47.

Interviews with 21 students who did not complete the program are examined. The primary source of dis-satisfaction expressed by students was their perception that faculty were not approachable.

Association of American Universities (AAU)
1990 "Institutional Policies to Improve Doctoral Education." A Policy Statement of the Association of American Universities and the Association of Graduate Schools in the AAU. Washington, DC: AAU.

Universities that have carried out comparative assessments of doctoral programs have found that departments with well-structured programs, clear expectations of graduate student performance and faculty responsibilities, and widely shared faculty commitments to encourage and facilitate students' progress have lower attrition rates and shorter times-to-degree than comparable departments whose programs lack those properties.

Bean, John P.

1980 "Dropouts and Turnover: The Synthesis and Test of a Causal Model of Student Attrition." *Research in Higher Education* 12 (2): 155-87.

Questionnaires were distributed to approximately 1,200 university freshmen to develop and test a causal model of student attrition. The causal model synthesized research findings on turnover in work organizations with student attrition from institutions of higher education.

Benkin, Ellen M.

1984 "Where Have All the Doctoral Students Gone? A Study of Doctoral Students' Attrition at UCLA." Ph.D. diss., University of California, Los Angeles.

The study focused on approximately 4,300 students who entered doctoral programs at UCLA in 1969, 1970, and 1971. The status of students was examined at the end of the 1981 spring term.

Blume, S., and O. Amsterdamska

1987 *Post-graduate Education in the 1980s.* Paris: Organization for Economic Cooperation and Development.

The report discusses graduate education (master's and doctoral) in countries having membership in the Organization for Economic Cooperation and Development (OECD), with particular attention on the duration of research training and the problem of non-completion. An important reason for not completing the dissertation was a poor working relationship with the advisor and/or committee (except for bioscientists). Data from telephone interviews with 25 former doctoral students in psychology, sociology, zoology, physics, electrical engineering, and biochemistry are included.

Bodian, Lester Hal

1987 "Career Instrumentality of Degree Completion as a Factor in Doctoral Student Attrition." Ph.D. diss., University of Maryland.

A theory of career instrumentality (the extent to which a doctoral student perceives that the completion of the degree is relevant to a career goal) is developed through a study of the literature on employee turnover and graduate attrition. Data from a survey of 670 Ph.D. students at the University of Maryland in 1986 is presented. Career motivation (a desire to enter the guild) is shown to affect student persistence in maintaining relationships with faculty members.

Bowen, William G., and Neil L. Rudenstine

1992 *In Pursuit of the PhD.* Princeton, NJ: Princeton University Press.

The study reviews data from ten leading research universities regarding the educational experiences of 35,000 graduate students in English, history, political science, economics, mathematics, and physics, as well as the graduate experiences of 13,000 winners of prestigious national fellowships. The authors conclude that there are opportunities to achieve significant improvements in the organization and functioning of graduate programs.

Burke, James D.

1983 "Chapel Hill, Berkeley Head Graduate Rankings." *Chemical and Engineering News* 61: 69.

Tabulation of degrees awarded in chemistry in 1981-82.

1984 "Urbana, Chapel Hill Top Graduate Rankings." *Chemical and Engineering News* 62: 43.

Tabulation of degrees awarded in chemistry in 1982-83.

1986 "Indiana New Leader of Graduate Listing." *Chemical and Engineering News* 64: 59.

Tabulation of degrees awarded in chemistry in 1984-85.

1988 "A Four-Year Model for the Ph.D. Degree Program in Chemistry." *Journal of Chemical Education* 65: 592-93.

The author notes that registered time-to-degree at his alma mater, the University of California at Berkeley, has increased from three and one-half years in the early 1960s to five years plus in the mid-1980s. He suggests a program design for degree completion in four years (emphasizing an early introduction to research and productivity), and the use of effective management practices, noting that there is extensive literature on the management of research. The article is based on the author's experience and offers a prescription for shorter time-to-degree in a graduate program in chemistry.

Cabrera, Alberto F., Maria B. Castaneda, Amaury Nora, and Dennis Hengstler

1992 "The Convergence Between Two Theories of College Persistence." *Journal of Higher Education* 63: 143-64.

The article examines evidence for the convergent and discriminant validity of V. Tinto's student integration model and J. Beans's model of student departure by tracking student outcomes of an entering freshman class (fall 1988) at a large southwestern institution.

Clark, Burton R.

1990 *The Research Foundations of Graduate Education: A Five-Country Exploration.* Washington, DC: Council of Graduate Schools.

The relationship of research to teaching and learning is at the heart of core problems in higher education. This cross-national analysis of other national systems of higher education allows for isolating some of the similarities and crucial differences in the system of American higher education.

Deck, Joseph C.

1982 "Chemistry Ph.D. Production in the United States." *Journal of Chemical Education* 59: 1002-04.

This study presents a tabulation of Ph.D. production by Roose-Andersen rankings, demonstrating that the best departments produce the most Ph.D.s.

Dolph, Robert F.
1983 "Factors Relating to Success or Failure in Obtaining the Doctorate." Ph.D. diss., Georgia State University.

This study presents the results of a survey of 266 doctoral students (145 Ph.D.s and 121 dropouts) enrolled between 1970 and 1980 in the program of educational administration at Georgia State University. Significant differences are shown between Ph.D.s (positive experience) and dropouts (negative experience) in faculty relationships.

Ehrenberg, Ronald G.
1991 "Academic Labor Supply." In *Economic Challenges in Higher Education, Part 2*, edited by Charles T. Clotfelter, Ronald G. Ehrenberg, Malcolm Getz, and John J. Siegfried. Chicago, IL: University of Chicago Press.

Data that were collected for a set of selected major universities during the 1970s and 1980s suggest that completion rates, while varying widely across fields and institutions, tend to lie in the 40 to 70 percent range.

Girves, Jean E., and Virginia Wemmerus
1988 "Developing Models of Graduate Student Degree Progress." *Journal of Higher Education* 59: 163-89.

This article proposes a model that links several variables to predict progress toward a graduate degree. Data were collected from a survey of 486 students entering at a major Midwestern university in the fall of 1977 and measured in 1984. Department characteristics were shown to be an important predictor of progress toward a degree, while the student's relationship with the advisor was found to be critical to graduate success.

Glover, Robert H., and Jerry Wilcox
1992 "An Interactive Model for Studying Student Retention." *AIR Professional File* 44 (Spring).

The authors present an overview of a design for improving the quality of information available for the continuous operational study of student retention at the University of Hartford. They address concerns about maintaining the confidentiality of files, while providing information to professional administrators, counselors, and faculty advisors.

Government-University-Industry Research Roundtable (GUIRR)
1992 *Fateful Choices. The Future of the U.S. Academic Research Enterprise. A Discussion Paper.* Washington, DC: National Academy Press.

This discussion paper examines recent trends affecting academic research in the U.S.; considers the impact of trends on the current academic research enterprise (the group of American universities and colleges performing significant research in the sciences and engineering); identifies longer-term issues that will affect the enterprise in the future; and explores ways in which the enterprise can meet future challenges.

Griskey, Richard G.
1990 "The Interrelationship of Faculty, Research Funds, and Doctoral Degrees." *Engineering Education* 80: 23-26.

This article discusses the relationships in engineering over an unspecified three-year period and provides a model for use in any engineering school.

Hauptman, Arthur M.
1986 *Students in Graduate and Professional Education: What We Know and Need to Know*. Washington, DC: Association of American Universities.

The study presents data from the National Center for Education Statistics, the U.S. Census Bureau, the NRC Doctorate Records File, and various federal departments for finishing graduate students in year groups from 1965 to 1983. It points out significant differences by field of study and type of financial support for graduate education. The results are divided among physical sciences, life sciences, and engineering; social sciences and humanities; education and professional; and others.

Herriott, Robert E.
1989 "A Survey of Recent Ph.D. Attrition Studies Conducted by AGS Institutions." Paper presented at the annual conference of the Association of Graduate Schools, Minneapolis, Minnesota.

The paper presents nine attrition studies, completed by members of the AGS, that indicate attrition is greater in the humanities and social sciences than in physical and biological sciences.

Hewitt, Nancy M., and Elaine Seymour
1991 *Talking About Leaving. Factors Contributing to High Attrition Rates Among Science, Mathematics & Engineering Undergraduate Majors. Final Report to the Alfred P. Sloan Foundation on Ethnographic Inquiry at Seven Institutions*. Boulder, CO: Bureau of Sociological Research, University of Colorado.

The report presents interviews with 149 current and former science, mathematics, and engineering (SME) students at seven institutions to elicit the range of factors which contribute to attrition from SME majors. Theories about the relative experiences of "switchers" and "non-switchers" are presented.

Heylin, Michael
1989 "Berkeley, Illinois Top Producers of Chemists." *Chemical and Engineering News* 67: 99.

Tabulation of degrees awarded in chemistry 1987-88.

Isaac, Paul D., Roy A. Koenigsknecht, Gary D. Malaney, and John E. Karras
1989 "Factors Related to Doctoral Dissertation Topic Selection." *Research in Higher Education* 30: 357-73.

This article explores the circumstances of selecting a dissertation topic and suggests that the dissertation may be a significant factor in lengthening time-to-degree. Data are derived from a survey of 438 finishing doctoral students at a major Midwestern research university in education, humanities, mathematics and physics, social and behavioral sciences, arts, engineering, business, agriculture, and biosciences from June 1986 to March 1987. Dissertation decisions affecting time-to-degree are shown to differ by field of study. The study also indicates that science students benefit from close faculty supervision by having a shorter time-to-degree than other students.

Jacks, Penelope, Daryl E. Chubin, Alan L. Porter, and Terry Connolly

1983   "The ABCs of ABDs: A Study of Incomplete Doctorates." *Improving College and University Teaching* 31: 74-81.

This study of former doctoral students in psychology, sociology, zoology, physics, electrical engineering, and biochemistry shows that the principal reasons for not completing their dissertation vary by field of study. The primary reason for failure to complete their program was a poor working relationship with the advisor and/or committee.

Jones, George Bryan, Jr.

1987   "Eleven Years of Admissions to the Temple University Ph.D. Program in Counseling Psychology, 1970-1980: A Study in Program Completion." Ph.D. diss., Temple University.

This study is based on a survey of 117 doctoral students (85 of whom earned the Ph.D.) at Temple University in 1986 and finds that that faculty management of student research is an important factor in degree completion or noncompletion.

Langenbach, Michael, and Lloyd Korhonen

1988   "Persisters and Nonpersisters in a Graduate-Level Nontraditional Liberal Education Program." *Adult Education Quarterly* 38 (3): 136-48.

This is an exploratory study of "persisters and nonpersisters" in a graduate-level, nontraditional liberal education program. Five demographic factors proved to be significant: age; type of bachelor's degree; years between completion of the bachelor's degree and enrollment in an M.A. degree program; site; and the social science score on the Undergraduate Assessment Program Test.

LeBlanc, Albert

1984   "The Challenge We Face with the Music Doctorate." *Music Educators Journal* 71: 34-37.

This article considers doctoral programs in music in a general period of decline in job opportunities. It recommends a reduction in program size while working to improve program quality.

Miselis, Karen L., William McManus, and Eileen Kraus

1991   "We Can Improve Our Graduate Programs: Analysis of Ph.D. Student Attrition and Time-to-Degree at the University of Pennsylvania." Paper presented at the Annual Forum of the Association of Institutional Research, San Francisco, California, May 29.

This paper describes efforts to build a data base from institutional files to analyze time-to-degree and Ph.D. completion rates in 32 graduate groups from students matriculating between the fall of 1973 and the spring of 1989.

National Research Council (NRC)

1990 *On Time to the Doctorate. A Study of the Increased Time to Complete Doctorates in Science and Engineering.* Washington, DC: National Academy Press.

This study presents an analysis of doctoral completion times since 1967. It provides a time-series data base for the period from 1967 to 1986 and develops a model that explains some of the factors that have been responsible for lengthening time-to-degree.

Nerad, Maresi

1991 *Doctoral Education at the University of California and Factors Affecting Time-To-Degree.* Oakland, CA: Office of the President, University of California.

The study reviews data from the National Research Council, from interviews with approximately 300 doctoral students, and from selected campuses of the University of California System to examine whether students took longer to complete their doctorates in the 1980s than they did 20 years earlier at the University of California. Factors that might account for observed differences are examined.

Nerad, Maresi, and Joseph Cerny

1991 "From Facts to Action: Expanding the Educational Role of the Graduate Division." *Communicator* (May Special Edition). Washington, DC: Council of Graduate Schools.

The study compares average time-to-degree in Ph.D. programs and completion rates at the University of California at Berkeley to national trends and similar analyses at comparable institutions. It finds (1) a wide variance in time-to-degree and completion rates by field of study and (2) shorter time-to-degree for students in engineering and natural sciences than for students in the humanities and social sciences. A similar variance for completion rates was noted. Poor communication and lack of guidance from faculty members were found to contribute to longer time-to-degree. The authors describe various research activities to address these issues, including quantitative analyses supplemented with qualitative methods to develop a basis for designing recommendations and programmatic outreach activities.

Organization for Economic Cooperation and Development (OECD)

1989 *Research Manpower: Managing Supply and Demand.* Paris: OECD.

Realizing the value of exchanging information on experience in the development of human resources for research and development, OECD organized a meeting of member countries to help them develop improved strategies and techniques for managing scientific and technological

42

development more efficiently. The various mechanisms which are involved in the education of research personnel are considered to form a dynamic system whose output is the flow of new personnel and whose behavior is affected by inputs, some of which are amenable to control.

Rawls, Rebecca L.
1987 "Facts and Figures for Chemical R&D." *Chemical and Engineering News* 65: 32-62.

Tabulation of research support in academic chemistry in 1985.

Rudd, Ernest
1985 *A New Look at Postgraduate Failure.* Guilford, England: SRHE & NFER-Nelson.

This study examines arguments of loss/gain by delay in achieving the doctorate, and it develops five groups of reasons for delay or noncompletion: (1) qualities of the student, (2) personal problems/accidents unrelated to their studies, (3) problems inherent in research, (4) personal academic problems, and (5) teaching and supervision. Recommendations pertaining to the organization of supervision are made. The data, measured as of 1966 on 1,008 students who entered doctoral study in 1957 and finished the doctorate in Britain, indicate that time-to-degree was shorter in science and technology groups than in social studies, languages, literature and area studies, and other arts groups.

1986 "The Drop-Outs and the Dilatory on the Road to the Doctorate." *Higher Education in Europe* 11 (4): 31-36.

The study looks at the problem of attrition and time-to-degree in Britain. Supervision of graduate work is identified as a major problem.

Science and Engineering Research Council and Social Science Research Council
1983 *Interdisciplinary Research Selection, Supervision and Training.* Brighton, England: University of Sussex.

This study presents data from a survey of 190 doctoral students in Britain who completed their Ph.D.s in 1978-79 in engineering, science, and social science. It found that time-to-degree is higher in social science than in engineering and science, and almost half of the sample cited difficulties with faculty supervision of students' research.

Tidball, M. Elizabeth
1986 "Baccalaureate Origins of Recent Natural Science Doctorates." *Journal of Higher Education* 57: 606-20.

The study discusses two findings: (1) that 288 undergraduate programs account for a majority of doctoral graduates in the natural sciences; and (2) that colleges are more productive than universities (private more productive than public), and that private colleges are more productive than private universities.

Tinto, Vincent

1982 "Limits of Theory and Practice in Student Attrition." *Journal of Higher Education* 53 (6): 687-700.

The author reviews the limits of the research and theory dealing with undergraduate student attrition.

1991 "Toward a Theory of Graduate Persistence." Paper presented at the annual meeting of the American Educational Research Association, Chicago, Illinois.

Data from the literature are presented, showing that field of study has greater influence on doctoral persistence than the institution. The faculty-mentor relationship is also shown to be a major factor in degree completion.

Tuckman, Howard P., Susan Coyle, and Yupin Bae

1989 "The Lengthening of Time to Completion of the Doctorate Degree." *Research in Higher Education* 30: 503-16.

The study discusses how time-to-degree has increased in 11 scientific and engineering fields, indicating the differences and increases and calling for further research on cause. Data from the NRC Doctorate Records File for 1967, 1977, and 1987 in physical sciences, biological sciences, and social sciences are presented, showing a greater increase in time-to-degree for social sciences than for physical and biological sciences.

U.S. Congress, Office of Technology Assessment

1988 *Educating Scientists and Engineers: Grade School to Grad School.* OTA-SET-377. Washington, DC: U.S. Government Printing Office.

This report examines the forces associated with elementary and secondary education that shape the talent pool; traces pathways to undergraduate and graduate education in science and engineering; and presents a discussion of policy areas for possible congressional action developed under two strategies labeled "retention" and "recruitment."

1989 *Higher Education for Science and Engineering—A Background Paper.* OTA BP-SET-52. Washington, DC: U.S. Government Printing Office.

The paper looks at American colleges and universities as producers of a future work force and provides a perspective on fledgling scientists and engineers, focusing on the endpoint of educational preparation—undergraduate and graduate study—for science and engineering careers.

Valentine, Nancy L.

1987 "Factors Related to Attrition from Doctor of Education Programs." Paper presented at annual meeting of the Association of Institutional Research, Kansas City, Missouri, May 3-6.

This paper is a study of completers and noncompleters of Ed.D. at West Virginia University and shows that recipients of the degree are more

44

likely to have positive relationships with faculty.

Zetterblom, Goran

1986 "Postgraduate Education in Sweden: Reforms and Results." *European Journal of Education* 21: 261-73.

This narrative discusses problems experienced in time to doctoral degree in Sweden and steps taken. It found that long study periods and high dropout rates led to the improvement of student grants. Concomitantly, time limits were tightened up, and admission qualifications were made more stringent. Data are derived from Swedish literature. Disciplinary differences in the conduct of graduate study are noted. The study found there is less attrition and shorter time-to-degree in the natural sciences than in the humanities and social sciences and that strong faculty supervision results in lower attrition and time-to-degree in the sciences.

Zwick, Rebecca

1991 *An Analysis of Graduate School Careers in Three Universities: Differences in Attainment Patterns Across Academic Programs and Demographic Groups.* Princeton, NJ: Educational Testing Service.

Data on 4,637 doctoral students entering at three major research universities from 1978 to 1985 in chemistry, English, history, mathematics, political science, psychology, economics, philosophy, physics, computer science, and sociology indicated that doctoral candidacy is achieved earliest in chemistry, mathematics, physics, and computer science; next in psychology, political science, sociology, and economics; latest in history, English, and philosophy.

Zwick, Rebecca, and Henry I. Braun

1988 *Methods for Analyzing the Attainment of Graduate School Milestones: A Case Study.* GRE Board Professional Report No. 86-3P. Princeton, NJ: Educational Testing Service.

Data measured in 1987 on 1,379 doctoral students entering Northwestern University from 1972 to 1978 in psychology, chemistry, English, history, mathematics, political science, chemical engineering, economics, philosophy, physics, sociology, theatre, and computer science show that attrition appears to be highest in English, history, political science, economics, and philosophy.

APPENDIX A

DATA BASES FOR STUDIES
OF GRADUATE EDUCATION IN THE UNITED STATES

As part of its study, the panel contracted with the Commission on Professionals in Science and Technology in Washington, D.C., to update the 1984 *Guide to Data on Scientists and Engineers* (B. M. Vetter and S. Jensen-Fisher). The panel requested material summarizing data bases that "permit analysis of patterns of graduate attrition/degree attainment in the sciences and humanities." More specifically, the panel asked for a technical summary which would (1) focus on extant data bases, (2) identify measures available in each data base, (3) describe the format in which the data are available to education researches (tabular, tape, computer diskette), and (4) identify the source of the data base and update pattern. Subsequently, project staff circulated the summary prepared by the Commission to the various program contacts for technical verification and updating. The product of that effort follows.

How to Use the Appendix

The data bases included in this appendix have been listed alphabetically by the name of the sponsoring organization. A brief description of the data base, together with a list of available publications is provided. If more than one survey is included in the data base, each is described. The description includes information on survey methodology, population base, sampling procedure, and response rate. Variables included in the data base are also described.

Researchers interested in using the data bases listed in this appendix are encouraged to request, in writing, their data needs by addressing the contacts listed in the pages that follow.

It is possible this summary of available data bases has overlooked important information sources that would also serve the data needs of education researchers. To the proprietors of those data bases, we extend our apologies. Nonetheless, we believe we have captured in this appendix the majority of available data bases that, properly manipulated, can extend our understanding of patterns of graduate attrition and degree completion in the sciences and humanities.

American Geological Institute 4220 King Street Alexandria, VA 22302-1502	Contact:	Nick Claudy Tel: (703) 379-2480 Fax: (703) 379-7563 e-mail: nclaudy@agi.umd.edu

■ GEOSCIENCE STUDENT ENROLL-MENT AND DEGREES SURVEY

An annual survey of all U.S. Geoscience Departments that has been carried out since 1956. The return rate averages about 70 percent.

• DATA

Demographic: Sex, race/ethnicity, and citizenship.

Enrollments: By year in college, M.A./M.S. candidates and Ph.D. candidates by sex, and 12[*] field breakouts. Beginning with the early 1980s, minority enrollments have been collected for three major fields plus "other."

Foreign enrollments were collected by ten world areas of origin in 1990, with no subfield data. Beginning in 1990-91, foreign student survey showed 12 field breakouts by sex and type of visa.

Degrees: Level, including two-year degrees, for 12 field breakouts by sex, 3 field breakouts by minority, and 12 field breakouts for foreign graduates.

• AVAILABILITY

The data are published annually by the American Geological Institute, other geoscience organizations, and industry. Funding for the survey is from AGI.

---

[*]Beginning with the 1993-94 academic year, field breakouts expanded to 20 for total enrollments/degrees granted and for foreign enrollments/degrees. Ethnic-minority student enrollments/ degrees granted remain as three breakout fields plus "other."

American Institute of Physics	Contacts:	Patrick J. Mulvey
One Physics Ellipse		Tel: (301) 209-3076
College Park, MD 20740		Fax: (301) 209-0843
		Michael Neuschatz
		Tel: (301) 209-3077
		Fax: (301) 209-0843

The AIP is an umbrella society incorporating ten national societies in physics and astronomy, 19 affiliated societies, and student members. Many of its surveys dealing with graduate education and degrees are long-term annual surveys that began in the 1960s.

■ SURVEY OF ENROLLMENTS AND DEGREES

Both astronomy and physics departments are surveyed, and the survey results are displayed in three reports: *Enrollments and Degrees Report, Bachelor's Degree Recipients Report,* and *Graduate Student Report.*

• DATA

Enrollments: Undergraduate majors by year of study. First year (beginning) graduate students and total graduate students by attendance status and citizenship. Also collect information on total enrollments in introductory physics courses that is based on the amount of mathematics required for enrollment.

Degrees: Numbers of bachelor's, terminal master's, master's en route to a Ph.D., and Ph.D.s by sex, citizenship, and race/ethnicity of U.S. students.

• AVAILABILITY

The annual eight-page report summarizes the results of the survey. Single copies are free and available from the AIP.

American Institute of Physics One Physics Ellipse College Park, MD 20740	Contacts:	Patrick J. Mulvey Tel: (301) 209-3076 Fax: (301) 209-0843 Michael Neuschatz Tel: (301) 209-3077 Fax: (301) 209-0843

■ **GRADUATE STUDENT SURVEY**

Both physics and astronomy students are surveyed, and the results are reported separately in the same publication.

• **DATA**

Demographic: Sex, date of birth, citizenship, and racial/ethnic group.

Education: Degree(s) held by month and year of receipt, field and institution, and current study institution. Candidates for terminal master's, master's en route to Ph.D., Ph.D., or no degree program. Attendance status, full-time years of graduate study completed, major source of support, area of concentration, and types of research. For those earning or expecting to earn a degree in the current academic year, the specific degree and date to be conferred, and the student's plans after completion of that degree. Also included are the number of firm job offers received and expected for post-degree employment.

Employment: Full or part-time, U.S. or foreign, temporary or potentially permanent, type of employer, principal work activity, use of physics/astronomy training in job, date current employment began, and annual salary.

• **AVAILABILITY**

The annual 12-page report summarizes the results of the survey. Single copies are free and available from the AIP.

American Institute of Physics
One Physics Ellipse
College Park, MD 20740

Contacts: Patrick J. Mulvey
Tel: (301) 209-3076
Fax: (301) 209-0843

Michael Neuschatz
Tel: (301) 209-3077
Fax: (301) 209-0843

■ SURVEY OF PHYSICS AND OF ASTRONOMY BACHELORS

Both astronomy and physics students are surveyed, and the survey results are reported separately in the same publication.

• DATA

Demographic: Sex, race/ethnicity, citizenship, and type of high school physics taken. A series of questions ask what prompted the student's interest in physics, if the degree is a double major and in what, if a part-time student in his or her senior year, and whether the student's education began at a two-year institution.

Education: Date and institution of bachelor's degree, and whether the degree was a B.S. or a B.A. Postbaccalaureate plans include graduate study in physics or in something else. Those planning physics graduate study are asked where they will attend, and whether they will attend on a full or part-time basis. Those entering another field are also asked what they plan to study. All are asked their major source of support.

Employment: Employment status, plus how many firm offers were received in connection with the bachelor's degree. Current status of employment, whether it is temporary or potentially permanent, U.S. or foreign, the date employment began, and type of employer. Use of physics or astronomy training in work activity, principal activity, annual salary, and whether future graduate study is planned in one year or possibly later (and, if so, in what discipline), or not at all.

• AVAILABILITY

The annual eight-page report summarizes the results of the survey. Single copies are free and available from the AIP.

American Institutes for Research Project TALENT Data Bank P. O. Box 1113 Palo Alto, CA 94302	Contact:	Lauri Steel Tel: (415) 493-3550 Fax: (415) 858-0958

■ **Project TALENT**

A 1960 longitudinal study of a national probability sample of 375,000 students in grades 9-12. Follow-up surveys were conducted periodically through 1975. On the 11-year follow-up, overall response rates averaged 23 percent, while response rates for targeted follow-up samples averaged 77 percent.

• **DATA**

Social/Demographic: Sex, race, age, family composition, family size, birth order, education and occupation of mother and father, SES.

Cognitive/Social Psychological: Cognitive skills (23 tests, 14 scales), information (37 scales), personality traits (13 scales), interests (18 scales), educational and occupational plans and aspirations.

Education: High school completion, diploma, courses taken, grades, occupational preparation. College attendance, school attended, date of completion, degree(s) and highest level reached, major/minor fields, grades/units earned, financing, occupational preparation. Non-college postsecondary program attendance, type of program, occupational preparation, license/certificate(s) earned. Graduate school attendance, school attended, date of completion, degree(s) earned, major/minor fields.

Employment: For each follow-up employment status, work experience, current occupation, earnings, job satisfaction (overall, 16 dimensions), career plans, and military service.

Other Personal: Marital status, marital history, number and ages of children, spouse's education/ occupation, health, quality of life (overall, 15 dimensions).

• **AVAILABILITY**

A 4,000 case public use file may be obtained from the data archive at the Inter-University Consortium for Political and Social Research at the University of Michigan. Other files may be obtained, at cost, directly from the Project TALENT Data Bank.

American Mathematical Society P.O. Box 6248 Providence, RI 02940	Contact:	Kinda Remick Tel: (800) 321-4267 Fax: (401) 455-4004 e-mail: survey@ams.org

■ ANNUAL AMS-IMS-MAA SURVEY

• Departmental Profile Survey

AMS has surveyed departments of the mathematical sciences each year since 1957. The survey did not include information on graduate students prior to 1970 when questions on enrollments by course, departmental size, and teaching load were added. The annual survey—carried out by AMS for itself, the Mathematical Association of America, and the Institute of Mathematical Statistics—now requests the total enrollment in undergraduate and graduate mathematical sciences courses. Also requested are the number of full-time graduate students and the number of full-time first year students by citizenship and sex. The number of junior and senior undergraduate majors, by sex, is also requested for the current and previous fall.

Full-time faculty information includes whether tenured or untenured (if tenure eligible) and the number of full-time faculty not eligible for tenure track, by sex, and whether doctoral or non-doctoral for the current and previous fall. Numbers of part-time faculty also are requested by sex and the highest degree for both years. Other questions ask for the number of full-time faculty in the previous fall term who retired and the number who died, the number of full-time doctoral faculty positions they tried to fill for the current academic year, how many of them were tenured or tenure-eligible positions, and

how many were open to new doctoral recipients. Finally, the questionnaire asks for results of the hiring attempts in terms of hires by sex, whether doctoral or nondoctoral, and the number of positions still unfilled. Some surveys for earlier years requested information on graduate student support. This part of the survey is sent to all college and university mathematical sciences departments (about 1,570 U.S. departments) and provides no useful information relative to graduate retention.

• Survey of Salaries and Professional Experience of New Doctorates/Doctorates Granted Survey

Carried out each year, the survey examines the numbers and some demographic characteristics of new doctoral recipients, including sex, type of granting institution, citizenship, and race/ethnicity. Employment and salary information are also obtained. It may be possible to compare the graduate enrollment data with new doctorates by institution.

Findings are published in *NOTICES of the AMS*. Not available on tape.

• Faculty Salary Survey

This annual survey collects faculty salaries, by rank, in departments of mathematical sciences in the U.S.

American Political Science Association 1527 New Hampshire Avenue, NW Washington DC 20036	Contact:	Michael Brintnall Tel: (202) 483-2512 Fax: (202) 483-2657

■ ANNUAL SURVEY OF DEPART-MENTS OF POLITICAL SCIENCE

The survey reports on departments, degree awards by level, staff size and characteristics, historical changes, faculty hires and losses, departmental resources, and required courses.

■ GRADUATE STUDENTS AND FACULTY

• DATA

Students by Graduate Program Level: Applicants (entering and continuing), enrollments by sex, race, Latino origin, citizenship, and school.

Departments awarding graduate degrees report graduate student admissions, acceptances, enrollments, and degree awards.

Faculty by Graduate Program Level: Numbers by school, rank, sex, tenure status, citizenship, race, Hispanic origin. Departures by reason for leaving and new type of employer, new hires by reason for opening, rank and tenure status by sex and race, number of applicants for positions filled, expected hires in coming year, and salary ranges by rank and sex.

Departmental Characteristics: Control, size, total enrollment, number, level and names of degrees awarded. Size and distribution of staff by rank and tenure status. Departmental travel funds, requirements to use departmental travel funds, funds from grants and contracts, secretarial personnel. Number of undergraduate majors and whether the number is rising or falling, credit hours and courses required for major. Teaching load of faculty, salary budget, salaries ($1,000 increments) by rank and sex, average fringe benefits, salary, degree level and teaching experience of new hires last year, and median salary of black faculty, if any, by rank.

• AVAILABILITY

Published in *Departmental Services Program: 1990-91 Survey of Departments*. A new edition is published each spring. Summary tables are published in the American Political Science Association's journal, *PS*.

A second report is *Graduate Students and Faculty in Political Science Ph.D. and M.A. Programs 1991*. No data tapes are available.

American Psychological Association
Research Office
750 First Street, NE
Washington, DC 20002

Contact: Jessica Kohout
Tel: (202) 336-5980
Fax: (202) 336-6148

■ BIENNIAL SURVEY OF GRADUATE DEPARTMENTS OF PSYCHOLOGY

Begun in 1978, this survey requests information on departmental characteristics, faculty characteristics and salaries, and data on students (particularly full-time doctoral students) and their support. Data on such issues as enrollments, graduate curriculum, and departmental policies and activities are collected periodically as need arises. Sex and race of graduate students, salaries of faculty, and other departmental variables are collected in some but not in all years. Form requests estimate of time to complete survey. Attrition questions are not asked in each mailing but are repeated periodically.

• METHODOLOGY

The survey is mailed to all departments listed in the most recent edition of *Graduate Study in Psychology*. In 1991, departments in associated fields were dropped from this publication, but they are still surveyed by ODEER. In the 1993-94 survey 581 U.S. and 34 Canadian departments were surveyed. The response rate for U.S. doctorate universities was 73 percent for public institutions and 70 percent for private institutions. Response rates for master's departments were 64 percent and 65 percent, respectively. The total U.S. response rate was 69 percent. The

1991-92 survey did include extensive questions on attrition and retention.

• DATA

1991-92 Survey: Departmental characteristics, degrees awarded, detail of program subfields offered. Students enrolled by year in program, attendance status, broad field, and financial support. There is also a special section on graduate student applications, enrollments, retention, and attrition.

Faculty: Tenured, tenure track and other faculty, salaried, and paid per course. Number of new full-time regular faculty.

1990-91 Survey: Departmental characteristics, degrees awarded, detail of program subfields offered. Students enrolled by year in program, attendance status, broad field, and financial support. Special section on departmental and institutional resources for research and support services.

Faculty: Tenured, tenure track and other faculty, salaried, and paid per course. Number of new full-time regular faculty in the fall of 1989 or in January 1990 by rank at hire, components of hiring package such as travel funds, summer salary, research equipment, space renovation, and approximate cost of each.

1989-90 Survey: Departmental characteristics, degrees awarded, and detail of program subfields offered. Students enrolled by year in program, attendance status, and financial support. Drops traineeships as mechanism of support. Special

54

section on graduate courses and training in psychopharmacology, substance abuse, and basic science.

1988-89 Survey: Includes data on sex and race/ethnicity of students and faculty by rank and tenure status, as well as data requested in 1989-90. Degrees awarded, by level, and for doctorates by type of degree (Ph.D., Psy.D., Ed.D.). Graduate enrollments in doctoral programs by attendance status. Full-time students by subfield, year in program (first year and beyond first year), type of support (TA, RA, fellowship), stipend, tuition coverage for 9 or 12 months, expected hours/week for TA and RA. Level of support for part-time students. The same information is requested for master's students.

Departmental applications and retention statistics, requirements for admission, whether a face-to-face or phone interview is required, who does the interviewing, and cost reimbursement for students doing face-to-face interviews. Number of students who applied, number who were accepted, and number who enrolled by subfield and type of program (master's or Ph.D.). Attrition data for students who began full-time doctoral programs in the fall of 1982 by asking how many started, how many have earned the Ph.D., how many are still enrolled, how many are working toward the Ph.D., and how many are not working toward the degree but have not formally left the program or have formally left without completing the Ph.D. The same current information was requested for master's entrants in the fall of 1985.

1987-88 Survey: Details graduate enrollments by program, degree sought, race/ethnicity, sex, attendance status, support by year in graduate school, hours required for Tas and RAs. Faculty by tenure status, new and replacement positions, departures and retirements by reason, source of new full-time regular faculty, and details of tenure and retirement policies. Departmental administration structure and salaries.

1986-87 Survey: Usual departmental characteristics; number, type of support, and level of support for students (by year) in graduate school and degree program. Source of faculty research grants. Details by rank, faculty teaching loads by hours spent, courses taught, other duties, and research grants/ contracts. Full range of faculty positions and salaries, including department chair and other administrators such as director of clinical training. Asks how raises were determined. Distinguishes new faculty, broken out by new Ph.D. and two years' postdoctoral experience. Same faculty detail as in previous year.

1985-86 Survey: Also asks master's applications and admissions for the fall of 1980 by program area. Distinguishes ABDs from other doctoral students. Compares time expended by TAs and RAs, includes support from traineeships, and delineates teaching responsibilities of all graduate students in the department. Requests information on departmental resources (secretaries/clerical staff, research support staff). Delineates tenure track and non tenure-track faculty by source of salary. Examines departmental budgets for travel, including source of funds and who used the funds. Departmental budget for operations, for acquiring or upgrading instructional and research equipment, for computer usage, and for other activities. External funds for research, training, or equipment. Detail of faculty salaries, including chair and other administrative positions. For each faculty member the subfield, employment status, rank and years in rank, sex, ethnicity/race, highest degree and year, tenure status, and salary.

• **AVAILABILITY**

Annual publication, i.e., *1989-90 Characteristics of Graduate Departments of Psychology*, 66 pp., January 1992. Not available on tape.

Association of American Universities Association of Graduate Schools Educational Testing Service Rosedale Road, MS 19-T Princeton, NJ 08541	Contact:	Rocco P. Russo Tel: (609) 734-5361 Fax: (609) 734-5010 e-mail: ags_project@ets.org

■ AAU/AGS PROJECT FOR RESEARCH ON DOCTORAL EDUCATION

A longitudinal data base relevant to the flow of individuals into and through Ph.D. programs in 10 fields: biochemistry, chemical engineering, economics, English, history, mathematics, mechanical engineering, physics, political science, and psychology (excluding clinical and counseling). Institutional data sets about applicants and students are transferred annually by approximately 40 (ultimately 60) major research universities. A record is maintained for all applicants to and students in any of the selected graduate programs, including multiple applications. Since 1989 the project's research efforts have supported the annual collection, merging, analysis, and reporting of data maintained by the project via a standardized, longitudinal multi-institutional data base.

Data sets maintained by the project are designed to support analytic summaries by doctoral program for selected individual groups. The analytic groups tabulated for the applicant data sets include applicants, accepted applicants, and enrolled applicants. The analytic groups tabulated for the student data sets include (1) stage 1 students (individuals who have been enrolled in a doctoral program for not more than one academic year and have not achieved candidacy), (2) stage 2 students (individuals who have been enrolled in a doctoral program for more than one academic year and have not achieved candidacy), (3) stage 3 students (individuals who have achieved candidacy but have not been awarded a Ph.D. degree), and (4) stage 4 students (individuals who have graduated with a Ph.D. degree). Related student groups which can be studied include (1) students who dropped out or ended their doctoral program studies prior to completion, (2) students who are not enrolled but are eligible to enroll or are on leave, and (3) students who have transferred to another program within the institution.

• DATA

Demographic: Gender, age, citizenship status, ethnic status.

Educational: Baccalaureate institution, admission decision, enrollment decision, enrollment status, candidacy status, GRE scores, financial aid data.

• AVAILABILITY

Annual reports to participating institutions, allowing comparisons with other institutions of similar characteristics and special topic reports and bulletins. A publication list is available. Several existing data sets are available for analysis, including a longitudinal student data base that maintains the student records linked annually from the fall of 1989 through the fall of 1992.

Commission on Professionals in Science and Technology 1333 H Street, NW, Suite 112 Washington DC 20005	Contact:	Eleanor Babco Tel: (202) 326-7080 Fax: (202) 842-1603 e-mail: ebabco@aaas.org

■ **FEDERAL SUPPORT FOR SCIENCE AND ENGINEERING EDUCATION**

The unpublished report "Federal Support for Science and Engineering Education: Effect on Output of Scientists and Engineers, 1945-1986" was prepared in 1987 under contract with the Office of Technology Assessment (Project Officer, Daryl Chubin). This report examines education expenditures in constant (1982) and current dollars, by source (federal agencies broken out), compared with degrees (1950-1984) by field, level, and sex (and by race/ethnicity on Ph.D.s after 1975). Enrollment of full-time graduate students in doctoral departments by field from 1965 through 1984 (also by sex after 1972), with the number and percent of students who had federal support each year. Graduate enrollment by S/E field and citizenship from 1965-1984. Science and engineering graduate students with federal support are compared with S/E Ph.D. awards, by field, for the years 1966-1984. Type of support (fellowship/ traineeship, RA, TA, other) of full-time S/E graduate students in Ph.D. departments for 1965-1984, and type of federal support for 1967-84. Source of support of full-time S/E graduate students in Ph.D. departments by sex, 1972-1984. Federal support by agency and field, 1969-1984. Finally, looking back from the Ph.D., the primary source of support by sex and citizenship, 1977-1985; primary federal support by field, sex, and citizenship, 1977-1985; and all federal support by sex and citizenship, 1972-1985.

• **AVAILABILITY**

All of the many tables have been graphed, so that changes over time and by field or by sex can be readily seen. Only one copy of this very long report exists at CPST, and, presumably, one exists at OTA. The data were compiled year by year from published and unpublished reports from the National Research Council, the National Science Foundation, the Department of Education, and several other federal agencies. A list of pertinent (and still unanswered) questions is appended at the end of the 41 pages of text that explains and expands on the study's findings.

The Computing Research Association	Contact:
Suite 718	Tel: (202) 234-21
1875 Connecticut Avenue, NW	Fax: (202) 667-1066
Washington, DC 20009	e-mail: survey@cra.org

■ CRA TAULBEE SURVEY

This is an annual survey honoring the late Orrin E. Taulbee who conducted the survey from 1970 until 1984. For the 1995 survey, questionnaires were sent to all computing departments in the Forsythe list, comprising 162 Ph.D.-granting departments in the U.S. and Canada—149 in computer science (some also include computer engineering) and 13 in computer engineering only. The survey focuses on Ph.D. production, graduate student enrollment, and faculty. The survey is sent at the beginning of the fall semester and usually results in a response rate above 90 percent. Changes in the questionnaire, response rate, and survey methodology over the years have rendered historical comparisons somewhat problematic, but they are still useful in certain cases.

• DATA

Demographic: Sex, race, ethnicity, disability, and residency status.

Education: Number of departments, number of Ph.D. awards (by NRC department rank), projected number of Ph.D.s to be awarded next year, number of bachelor's and master's degrees awarded by Ph.D.-granting departments. Number of Ph.D.s enrolled, number of newly enrolled undergraduate and graduate students, number of Ph.D. students who have passed their qualifying exams, and number of newly enrolled Ph.D. students who have a bachelor's degree in computer science or computer engineering.

Employment: Employment status, type of employer, and field specialty of students awarded Ph.D.s. Number and rank of faculty, tenure status. Number of postdoctorates, non-teaching research faculty, non-tenure-track faculty, and other faculty such as visitors. Number of faculty newly hired, number of faculty who left (because of death, retirement, change), and projected faculty growth. Also, faculty salaries broken down by NRC department rank and faculty rank with minimums, means, and maximums.

• AVAILABILITY

Results of the survey are published in *Computing Research News* and on CRA's web site (http://www.cra.org). The 1995 survey appears in the March 1996 issue of *Computing Research News*. Raw data is not currently made available, although CRA may publish a certain subset of raw data on its web site, which should be checked from time to time for the most up-to-date information.

Council of Graduate Schools Suite 430, One Dupont Circle, NW Washington, DC 20036-1173	Contact:	Peter D. Syverson Tel: (202) 223-3791 Fax: (202) 331-7157
Graduate Records Examinations Program Educational Testing Service Princeton, NJ 08541-6000	Contact:	Jacqueline B. Briel Tel: (609) 951-1545

■ THE CGS/GRE SURVEY OF GRADUATE ENROLLMENT

Since 1986 the Council of Graduate Schools and the Graduate Records Examinations Board have conducted an annual survey of graduate enrollment and degrees at the approximately 660 institutions that are members of the Council or its regional affiliates.

• METHODOLOGY

The survey is conducted each winter. Institutions provide data on graduate enrollment and applications for the fall term and data on degrees conferred during the previous (12-month) school year. Total data, as well as data from up to 51 individual disciplines, are collected from each institution. Consistently, more than 90 percent of the institutions complete and return the survey.

• DATA

Enrollment: Includes enrollment by gender, ethnicity, citizenship, enrollment status (full-time and part- time), and first-time enrollment for the fall term.

Applications: Includes the number of complete applications submitted for the fall term, applications accepted, and applications not accepted.

Degrees: Includes number of master's and doctoral degrees conferred by gender.

• REPORTING

The data are cross-referenced by institutional variables such as public or private affiliation, highest degree granted, and institution-type categories based on the Carnegie classification system. Discipline data are grouped into nine broad fields plus "other." Trends in graduate enrollment and degrees since 1986 are reported in addition to the single-year data.

• AVAILABILITY

Survey results are published in the annual *Graduate Enrollment and Degrees* which is available from CGS. Early release data and special reports are also published in the Council's newsletter, the *CGS Communicator*. Data from earlier survey years, as well as appendices providing taxonomies, response rates, and other information, are available from the GRE Program in their *Annual Report*.

U.S. Department of Education	Contact:	Aurora M. D'Amico
Office of Educational Research		Tel: (202) 219-1365
and Improvement		Fax: (202) 219-1529
555 New Jersey Avenue, NW		e-mail: Aurora_D'Amico@ed.gov
Washington DC 20208-5570		e-mail: adamico@inet.ed.gov

■ NATIONAL LONGITUDINAL STUDIES

Four longitudinal survey groups make up the program: NLS-72, High School and Beyond—1980 Senior Cohort and 1980 Sophomore Cohort, and NELS-88 eighth graders (although the latter is not yet relevant to the subject of this report).

■ NATIONAL LONGITUDINAL SURVEY OF THE HIGH SCHOOL SENIORS OF 1972 (NLS-72)

The Educational Testing Service conducted a base year survey in the spring of 1972. The sample was deeply stratified and included 1,200 schools with 18 seniors per school when school size permitted. A total of 19,001 students from 1,061 high schools provided base year data on up to three data collection forms: a Test Battery, a School Record Information Form, and a Student Questionnaire. The latter was completed by 16,683 seniors.

The first follow-up and the subsequent four follow-up surveys were conducted by Research Triangle Institute. The first, in October 1973, added 4,450 1972 seniors from 257 schools. Questions included location, current education, work, and/or training. The retention rate was 93.7 percent. The second follow-up in October 1974 requested similar

information at a new time point, but also included some new questions on work and education. The retention rate for the sample was 94.6 percent. A third follow-up in October 1976 obtained status in October 1976 as well as in the intervening year—October 1975—and summaries of experiences and activities since the previous follow-up. Retention was 93.9 percent.

The fourth follow-up in October 1979 updated work and educational history, and a subsample of 1,016 persons were retested on a subset of the base year test battery. Information on family formation and political participation was added. The response rate was 90.8 percent. The number of individuals with some key data elements for all time points is 16,450 (73 percent of respondents participating in at least one survey).

In 1984, NORC conducted the Postsecondary Education Transcript study, collecting transcripts from academic and vocational postsecondary institutions attended by respondents. Data can be merged with questionnaire data to support powerful quantitative analyses of the impacts of postsecondary schooling.

The fifth follow-up and its supplements were conducted by NORC in 1986, with questionnaires sent to a subsample of 14,489 members of the original 22,652 sample. Response rate was 89 percent. Respondents averaged 32 years of age and had been out of high school for 14 years. Retained in this sample were all Hispanics (728), teachers, and "potential teachers" (2,343) among the fourth follow-up participants. Outside sponsors added questions on marriage and family, graduate and professional school (principally MBA program) applications and plans, and teaching and attitudes toward teaching. (The Teaching Supplement is not included in the NICHD edition of the data tape, but attitudes toward the teaching profession are.)

The Postsecondary Transcript Study contains records for 12,599 individuals who entered and/or completed college or other kinds of postsecondary schools within 12 years of high school graduation. Although OERI would like to survey this group again at age 40, funds are not currently available

■ HIGH SCHOOL AND BEYOND

This survey began in 1980 by surveying 28,000 high school seniors and 30,000 sophomores. Follow-up surveys were conducted in 1982, 1984, and 1986 by NORC. The sample for each cohort was reduced by about half when sample members were two years out of high school. NORC conducted a survey of the 1980 sophomores in 1992. This follow-up study also collected postsecondary transcripts of all those who entered and/or completed college or other postsecondary programs.

■ NELS-88

Since this new sample starts with 1988 8th graders, it has no current application for the NRC study.

• AVAILABILITY

- All collected data are on CDS. The bibilography and publications are available on **Gopher@ed.gov**.

- The text file can be accessed on **gopher://gopher.ed.gov:10000/00/publications/elesec/long/nets/bibnels**.

- The compressed file is on **gopher://gopher.ed.gov:10000/59/publications/elesec/long/nels/nelsbib**.

U.S. Department of Education	Contact:	**Roslyn Korb**
National Center for Education Statistics		**Tel: (202) 219-1587**
Postsecondary Education Statistics Division		**e-mail:**
555 New Jersey Avenue, NW		**Roslyn_Korb@ed.gov**
Washington, DC 20208-5652		

■ **INTEGRATED POSTSECONDARY EDUCATION DATA SYSTEM**

NCES has established the Integrated Postsecondary Education Data System (IPEDS) as its core postsecondary education data collection program. It is a single, comprehensive system that encompasses all identified institutions whose primary purpose is to provide postsecondary education. IPEDS supersedes the Higher Education General Information Survey (HEGIS). From 1965 to 1986, data were collected via the HEGIS surveys only from institutions that were accredited at the college level by an accrediting organization recognized by the Secretary of the U.S. Department of Education.

IPEDS data provide a wealth of institutional-level data for analyzing the state of postsecondary education institutions. For example, IPEDS data can be used (with HEGIS data) to describe long-term trends in higher education.   The data necessary for conducting and interpreting special studies of postsecondary students, faculty, and staff are available within IPEDS. Using IPEDS data, policy makers and researchers can analyze postsecondary data on the number of students, graduates, first-time freshmen, and graduate and professional students by race/ethnicity and sex; the status of postsecondary vocational education programs; the number of individuals trained in certain occupational and vocational fields by sex, race/ethnicity, and level;   the   resources   generated   by postsecondary education; completions by type of program, level of award, race/ethnicity, and sex; and many other issues of interest.

• **METHODOLOGY**

Postsecondary education is defined within IPEDS as the provision of a formal instructional program whose curriculum is designed primarily for students who are beyond the compulsory age for high school. This includes academic, vocational, and continuing professional education programs, and excludes avocational and adult basic education programs. The following types of institutions are included within IPEDS: baccalaureate or higher degree-granting institutions, two-year award institutions, and less-than-two-year   institutions   (i.e., institutions whose awards usually result in terminal occupational awards or are creditable toward a formal two-year or higher award). Each of these three categories is further disaggregated by control (public, private nonprofit, and private for-profit), resulting in nine institutional categories or sectors.

Data are collected from approximately 11,000 postsecondary institutions. IPEDS has been designed to produce national, state, and institutional-level data for most postsecondary institutions.   However, only national-level estimates from a sample of institutions are available for the private, less-than-two-year institutions prior to 1993. Beginning with the 1993 survey year, institutional-level data are available for all postsecondary institutions eligible for federal student financial aid (Title IV) funding. For institutions not eligible under Title IV, only limited data will be requested through the Institutional Characteristics Survey.

• DATA

Institutional Characteristics: Address, congressional district, county, telephone number, tuition, control or affiliation, calendar system, levels of degrees and awards offered, types of programs, credit and contact hour data, and accreditation. Data are collected annually.

Fall Enrollment: Full and part-time enrollment by racial/ethnic category and sex for undergraduates, first-professional, and graduate students. Age distributions by level of enrollment and sex in odd-numbered years. First-time degree-seeking student enrollments by state of residence in even-numbered years.

Fall Enrollment in Occupationally Specific Programs: Fall enrollment in each occupationally specific program by sex and race/ethnicity in odd-numbered years.

Completions: Numbers of associate, bachelor's, master's, doctorate, and first-professional degrees, and other formal awards, by discipline and sex of recipient. Awards by racial/ethnic composition, program area, and sex are collected annually.

Salaries, Tenure, and Fringe Benefits of Full-Time Instructional Faculty: Full-time instructional faculty by rank, sex, tenure status, length of contract, salaries, and fringe benefits. Data are collected annually.

Financial Statistics: Current fund revenues by source (e.g., tuition and fees, government, gifts); current fund expenditures by function (e.g., instruction, research); assets and indebtedness; and endowment investments. Data are collected annually.

College and University Libraries: Number of branches, number and salaries of full-time equivalent staff by position. Circulation and interlibrary loan transactions, book and media collections, public service hours and number served, and operating expenditures by purpose. Data are collected in even-numbered years (see description in chapter 8).

Fall Staff: Number of institutional staff by occupational activity, full and part-time status, sex, and race/ethnicity. Data are collected in odd-numbered years. Beginning with 1993, this survey replaces the EEO-6 survey conducted by the Equal Employment Opportunity Commission.

• AVAILABILITY

NCES constituents with access to the Internet can tap a rich collection of education-related information at the U.S. Department of Education's (ED) public Gopher/FTP/World Wide Web site:

- A Gopher client, **gopher.ed.gov**, or select North America→U.S. Department of Education. From the main gopher menu, NCES-produced information is available under Educational Research, Improvement and Statistics (OERI & NCES)/National Center for Education Statistics(NCES)/.

- An FTP client, ftp to **ftp.ed.gov**, log on anonymous.

- A World Wide Web client such as NCSA Mosaic or lynx point to URL = **http://www.ed.gov/**.

- Dial-in users can access much of the same information through the OERI Toll-Free Electronic Bulletin Board which provides on-line access to statistical data research findings, information about Department of Education programs, and, in some cases, full texts of departmental documents. Computer users can retrieve this information at any hour using a modem (at speeds up to 14400 baud) and calling **1-800-222-4922**. The local, direct number is **(202) 219-1511**.

- For further information on electronic access contact William Freund, PESD, NCES, 555 New Jersey Avenue, NW, Washington, DC 20208, **(202) 219-1373**.

Department of Education	Contact:	Vance Grant
National Center for Education Statistics	Tel:	(202) 219-1659
Integrated Postsecondary Education Data System	Fax:	(202) 219-1696
555 New Jersey Avenue, NW		
Washington, DC 20208-5641		

■ **ENROLLMENTS IN
HIGHER EDUCATION**

An annual survey of enrollments by sex, full-time or part-time, level, and institutional control in two and four-year colleges. First time and total enrollments are requested. Data have been collected by race and ethnicity since 1976. In recent years (1990-91) the race/ethnicity data have been collected each fall.

In 1987, 1989, 1991, and 1993, surveys of enrollments by age were carried out. This survey is expected to be repeated in odd-numbered years in the future.

Occasionally, and most recently in the fall of 1988, the enrollment data were collected by broad major field. There is no consistent pattern for repeating that part of the enrollment survey.

■ **DEGREES AND OTHER
FORMAL AWARDS CONFERRED**

An annual survey of degree awards by level (including those requiring less than four years), sex, and fine field. In past odd-numbered years—1976-77 through 1988-89—the degree survey included the race/ethnicity of recipients in 30 broad fields. Beginning in 1988-89, the race/ethnicity data have been collected annually.

U.S. Department of Education	Contact:	Peter Stowe
National Center for Education Statistics		Tel: (202) 219-2009
Integrated Postsecondary Education Data System		Fax: (202) 219-1679
555 New Jersey Avenue, NW		e-mail:
Washington, DC 20208		Peter_Stowe@ed.gov

■ **RECENT COLLEGE GRADUATES STUDY**

This study of the employment and education experiences of recent college graduates has been conducted periodically since 1976. The sixth and last survey was conducted in 1991. The findings of that survey are summarized in "Occupational and Educational Outcomes of 1989-90 Bachelor's Degree Recipients 1 Year After Graduation: 1991." The study responds to a congressional mandate to determine the supply of new teachers in the job market by enumerating the supply of new teachers with a bachelor's or a master's degree. A publication based on the 1991 data and entitled *New Teachers in the Job Market, 1991 Update* summarizes the characteristics, certification, and teaching fields of bachelor's degree recipients who were new teachers in 1991. The 1987 survey collected transcript data on the bachelor's degree sample in addition to graduates' responses to the questionnaire.

• **METHODOLOGY**

A two-stage sample design is employed to select a nationally representative sample of 16,000 bachelor's and 2,000 master's degree recipients. In the first stage, higher education institutions granting bachelor's or master's degrees are stratified by control and the number of degrees awarded to education majors. Within each of these four strata institutions are selected according to a measure of size (the number of bachelor's and master's degrees awarded). In the second stage students from the 400 institutions selected in the first stage are stratified by degree obtained and selected major fields of study, especially education. Within groups of major fields of study students are randomly selected with different sampling rates to oversample certain major fields of study. A ratio-estimation procedure is used to inflate the sample results to estimates applicable to the total number of graduates.

• **DATA**

Demographic data include age, sex, race/ethnicity, marital status, and number of dependents. Education data include degree, major field of study, financial aid received, further education aspirations. Post-degree activities include continuation with education, labor force status, employment status, salary, occupation, job characteristics.

• **AVAILABILITY**

The 1991 survey data are available on floppy disk and CD ROM. The above-mentioned publications are also available. Previous years' data are available on CD ROM.

U.S. Department of Education
National Center for Education Statistics
Postsecondary Education Statistics Division
555 New Jersey Avenue, NW
Washington, DC 20208-5652

Contact: **Paula R. Knepper**
Tel: (202) 219-1914

■ BACCALAUREATE AND BEYOND LONGITUDINAL STUDY

The Baccalaureate and Beyond Longitudinal Study (B&B) provides information concerning education and work experiences after completing the bachelor's degree. It continues to provide cross-sectional information one year after bachelor's degree completion (comparable to the Recent College Graduate Survey) as well as longitudinal data concerning entry into and progress through graduate-level education and the work force. A special emphasis of B&B is on those entering public service areas, particularly teaching.

B&B greatly expands the knowledge about persistence, progress, and attainment after entry into graduate education. It also directly addresses issues concerning entry into the work force and rates of return. Its unique contribution is the longitudinal perspective on the graduate education/work interaction and the longer range information concerning newly qualified teachers and their entry into and continuation in the field. Questions that B&B can address about access to graduate or professional programs include timing, the application process, and entry into the program. Attainment/outcome questions include completion time for the bachelor's degree, timing of entry into the work force, and the relationship of field of study to area of employment. B&B is also able to inform the rate of return questions, particularly those associated with immediate entry into the work

force after completion of the bachelor's degree, issues concerning the interaction between education and work, and issues associated with entry into public service areas such as teaching and relative career advancement.

• METHODOLOGY

B&B plans to follow each cohort over a 12-year period, allowing a unique opportunity to gather information concerning delayed entry into graduate-level education, times to completion of graduate education, and the interactions between work and education at the graduate level. The B&B is based on the National Postsecondary Student Aid Study (NPSAS). NPSAS is a large, nationally representative sample of institutions, students, and parents, providing a highly efficient and cost-effective way to identify a nationally representative sample of baccalaureate degree completers in PSE. By using NPSAS as the base year for B&B longitudinal studies, two additional advantages are realized. One, there is coordination between the recurring cross-sectional studies and the longitudinal studies, and two, there is coordination among the postsecondary longitudinal studies. The information collected through NPSAS allows for the accurate identification of baccalaureate degree completers. Further, data from all components of NPSAS (the Student Record Abstract, the Student Interview, and the Parent Survey) are available as base-year data for the B&B sample. New B&B cohorts will alternate with BPS in using NPSAS surveys as their base.

- **DATA**

About 11,000 students who completed their degree in the 1992-93 academic year were included in the first B&B: 93/94. NPSAS: 93 provides data for over 8,000 of their parents. Components include (a) Base Year (1992) data (NPSAS Student Record Abstract, NPSAS Student Interview data, and NPSAS Parent Survey data) and (b) B&B Follow-up Surveys.

Student Record Abstract: Indicates major field of study, type and control of institution, financial aid, cost of attendance, family income, sex, and race/ethnicity.

Student Interview: Includes undergraduate and major GPA, date of first enrollment, financial aid, loan burden for undergraduate education, activities related to selection and entry into graduate school, activities related to obtaining employment after graduation, qualifications to teach, current marital status, employment and income, demographic information, college experiences, and future expectations.

Parental Survey: Looks at race/ethnicity, marital status, age, level of education achieved, income, occupation, financial support provided to children, methods of financing student's PSE expenses, involvement in student's selection of graduate school, and involvement in the student's obtaining a job after graduation.

Follow-up Surveys: Will include entry into graduate school, persistence in enrollment, periods of attendance, graduate loan burden, academic progress, change in field of study, education-related experiences, financial aid, current family status, entry into the work force, employment related training, entry and persistence in teaching, community service, political participation, further education plans, and future expectations.

Erikson Biographical Institute, Inc.	Contact:	G. E. Erikson
167 Angell Street		Tel: (401) 863-3355
Providence, RI 02906		Fax: (401) 454-0417

■ BIOLOGICAL DATA BASE

A data base totaling 248,876 individuals, of whom 77 percent are living, 69 percent are American (58 percent are living Americans), 29 percent have Ph.D.s, and 52 percent are scientists.

• DATA

Date and place of birth and sex. Degrees by institution and date, broad field of degree (science, social science, or humanities), and employment. Can compare birth year and Ph.D. year over large time spans. It includes a chart starting in 1870 showing the number of the Ph.D.s in the sample who took 3 years, 4 years, 5 years, 6 years, and up to 19 years to get the Ph.D. after receiving a bachelor's degree. The chart is subdivided for scientists, social scientists, humanists and unknown degree field. Within the sciences, data are broken out by conventional fields, largely in the life sciences. Modal and mean time-to-degree are fairly constant (and low) for decades before rising during the past decade.

Also included are data relating to approximately 8,000 individuals who were graduate students when they entered the data base and for whom there is no record of Ph.D. completion. A test of some of these individuals indicates that perhaps one-third of them do have the Ph.D., while a large number of them did not complete the degree.

Harvard University Project Access	Contact:	Gerald Holton
Jefferson Laboratory		Tel: (617) 495-4474
Cambridge, MA 02138		Fax: (617) 495-0416
		e-mail:
		holton@physics.harvard.edu

■ PROJECT ACCESS: A STUDY OF ACCESS TO SCIENTIFIC RESEARCH

This study has two components. The first is a questionnaire study of access of women scientists and engineers to research careers. It is based on a sample of 803 scientists (295 women) who received prestigious postdoctoral fellowships—104 women are Bunting Institute Fellows and Finalists from the years 1961-1984; 239 are NRC Postdoctoral Associates (147 men, 92 women) from the years 1959-1986; and 460 are NSF Postdoctoral Fellows (361 men, 99 women) from the years 1955-1985. Response rates for those who were contacted was 53.3 percent for former Bunting Fellows and Finalists; 60.6 percent for former NSF Fellows (62.1 percent for men and 55.6 percent for women); and 82.1 percent for former NRC Associates (81.7 percent for men and 82.9 percent for women).

The second component is a study based on 200 open-ended interviews with a subsample of respondents (108 women, 92 men). This sample has many characteristics (and probably individuals) in common with the Erikson sample, including, as it does, highly prestigious scientists of both sexes who attained the doctorate.

• QUESTIONNAIRE DATA

Demographic: Sex, race, ethnicity, physical handicap and year of impairment, prolonged illness before age 21. Date of birth, citizenship (including naturalization and visa status), country of prior citizenship, year of naturalization, country of present citizenship, birth year and sex of siblings. Marital status when doctorate received (during first doctoral appointment and as of January 1, 1988), year of birth of children, number living with participant on January 1, 1988. Education level of spouse, mother, and father. Year of death of parents who died before subject was 21, and year of parental divorce.

Education: Graduate university, year and field of highest degree, total time to the doctorate from the baccalaureate. Time spent as a full-time student, a part-time student, or not working on the degree. History of assistantships held (research, teaching, none, or other) and period held (throughout graduate school, more than half time, about half time, or less than half time). How an assistantship helped or hindered professional development, debt at time of doctorate, funding sources for doctorate, source of any graduate fellowship, and employment status in year preceding highest degree award. Questions about principal dissertation advisor and about postdoctoral appointments (title, year(s) of application for and holding fellowship, where it was served, and characteristics of scientists on the staff of the institution with which individual may have been affiliated during the postdoctoral appointment). Whether additional postdoctoral appointments other than the award noted were sought and obtained, reasons for taking postdoctoral appointments, importance of fellowship in attainment of present position, and number of mentors during all postdoctoral appointments.

Employment: University research positions in addition to postdoctoral appointments, if any. Research fields (during Ph.D., while a fellow, and later). Whether now part of a scientific research team, and, if not, why not. Present employment status, type of organization, name of employer, location, date and month began, type of position held, academic rank, if any. Tenured, tenure track, or outside traditional academic structure, and year tenure received. Graduate students now supervised, time spent on various activities, federal support for research, salary, and employment plans (seeking new position, retired, planning move).

- **AVAILABILITY**

The final report to the National Science Foundation on the first *Project Access: A Study of Access of Women Scientists and Engineers to Research Careers* was published in March 1991. The report on the follow-up NSF grant was issued in August 1992. The major results of Project Access have been published in two books. G. Sonnert, with the assistance of G. Holton. *Gender Differences in Science Careers: The Project Access Study.* New Brunswick, NJ: Rutgers University Press, 1995. G. Sonnert, with the assistance of G. Holton. *Who Succeeds in Science? The Gender Dimension.* New Brunswick, NJ: Rutgers University Press, 1995. Arrangements might be made with the principal investigator to share data information. The data have been deposited at the Henry A. Murray Research Center, Radcliffe College, Cambridge, MA 02138.

National Research Council
Office of Scientific and Engineering Personnel
Room TJ2035
2101 Constitution Ave., NW
Washington, DC 20418

Contact: Peter Henderson
             Tel: (202) 334-3155
             Fax: (202) 334-2753
             e-mail:
             phdsurvy@nas.edu

■ SURVEY OF EARNED DOCTORATES
(aka Doctorate Records File [DRF])

Since 1958 this annual survey has provided a nearly 100 percent response from all new doctorate recipients in U.S. universities.

• METHODOLOGY

Questionnaires are distributed to graduate deans who supply them to graduates who have completed requirements for the doctorate. Rosters of recipients are compiled by NRC after receipt of the questionnaires and verification made with the doctorate institution.

• DATA

Demographic: Name (including maiden or former name), permanent address, Social Security number, place and date of birth, gender, marital status, citizenship, race/ethnicity (since 1973), physical handicap (since 1985), number of dependents, and parents' education level.

Education: History includes place and year of high school graduation, dates of attendance and graduation from all higher education institutions, major field, dissertation title and departmental classification, detailed sources and types of graduate support, employment status in preceding year, and postgraduation plans.

Beginning in 1987, the questionnaire asks how many years since first baccalaureate degree were spent as a full-time student. Also beginning in 1987, a question was added on the level of cumulative debt related to education.

• AVAILABILITY

The NRC publishes an annual *Summary Report* which currently includes seven appendix tables for the current year. They provide data on degrees by fine field, gender, race/ethnicity, and citizenship (U.S., permanent residents, and temporary visas); a statistical profile of Ph.D.s by broad field, gender, citizenship, and race/ethnicity; sources of support by broad field and gender; state of Ph.D. institution by broad field and gender; and institutional sources of doctorates by state and broad field. There are also two trend appendix tables that present data for the most recent 10-year period: number of Ph.D.s by fine field and number of doctorates by gender, race/ethnicity, and citizenship status.

National Research Council	Contact:	Peter Henderson
Office of Scientific and Engineering Personnel		Tel: (202) 334-3155
Room TJ2035		Fax: (202) 334-2753
2101 Constitution Ave., NW		e-mail:
Washington, DC 20418		phdsurvy@nas.edu

■ SURVEY OF DOCTORATE RECIPIENTS

(Survey of Doctoral Scientists and Engineers prior to 1977)

The Survey of Doctorate Recipients (SDR) is a longitudinal employment survey of a stratified random sample of doctorate recipients in the sciences, engineering, and the humanities. The survey has been conducted every two years since 1973 (humanities doctorates were added in 1977) by the National Research Council with support from the National Science Foundation, the National Endowment for the Humanities, and other federal sponsors. In 1993, the latest year for which data is available, the sample was composed of over 50,000 science/engineering doctorates and 10,000 humanities doctorates. The overall response rate was 87 percent. Survey estimates were based on doctorates who were 75 years of age or less and who were residing in the United States in April 1993.

• DATA

Demographic: Date of birth, sex, racial and ethnic identity, citizenship and visa type for foreign citizens, marital status, children by age grouping, and physical handicap status.

Education: Field, institution and year of the doctorate, and education history. Carnegie classification of institution and Jones-Lindzey reputational rating.

Employment: Employment status, full-time or part-time and reason, reason for being out of labor force, job search restrictions for those unemployed and seeking. Current employer (name, location, type of organization), employment field, reason for non-science employment, faculty rank and tenure status, primary and secondary work activity, years of work experience, sources of federal support, energy-related work experience, and annual salary.

• AVAILABILITY

The NRC publishes a profile report of humanities doctorates every two years, but it has not, since the early 1980s, published a similar report on science and engineering doctorates. Instead, the NSF publishes detailed statistical tables on selected characteristics of doctoral scientists and engineers. The NRC will run special tabulations on a cost-reimbursement basis. A public use tape is available. For information contact the National Science Foundation, Division of Science Resources Studies, (703) 306-1780.

National Science Foundation	Contact:	Mary J. Golladay
4201 Wilson Boulevard		Tel: (703) 306-1774
Arlington, VA 22230		Fax: (703) 306-0510
		e-mail: mgollada@nsf.gov

■ SURVEY OF GRADUATE SCIENCE AND ENGINEERING STUDENTS

An annual survey sent to all of the science and engineering graduate departments in some 604 institutions in the U.S. and outlying areas. From 1984 through 1987, the surveys were conducted on a stratified random sample with all Ph.D.-granting institutions and all Historically Black Colleges and Universities included in the certainty stratum. Estimates for the remaining master's granting institutions were made and then re-estimated in 1988 on the basis of 1983 and 1988 data.

• DATA

Number of graduate students in the department by attendance status, detailed form and source of support, sex, first year versus all years, race/ethnicity, and citizenship. Postdoctorates and non-faculty research staff are reported by total; type and source of support; sex; and how many hold M.D., D.O., D.D.S., or D.V.M. degrees. Departmental information includes name of institution, name of department or program, any change since previous year, highest degree granted, and name and title of person filling out form.

• AVAILABILITY

Data tables are provided by all available parameters to persons requesting them. Data are also available on the World Wide Web at **http://www.nsf.gov/sbe/srs/stats.htm**.

National Science Foundation **4201 Wilson Boulevard** **Arlington, VA 22230**	**Contact:** **John Tsapogas** **Tel:** **(703) 306-1776** **Fax:** **(703) 306-0508** **e-mail: jtsapoga@nsf.gov**

■ NATIONAL SURVEY OF RECENT COLLEGE GRADUATES

Conducted by a contractor for NSF (most recently the WESTAT), this biennial survey is sent to a sample of about 21,000 science and engineering graduates at the bachelor's and master's level during the previous two years. They are selected from lists provided by a set of selected universities and colleges. The survey is conducted using Computer Assisted Telephone Interviewing (CATI). A mail follow-up is made only for respondents who prefer to submit responses in writing. The response rates over the last two survey cycles have been over 85 percent.

• DATA

Demographic: Sex, date and place of birth, citizenship and visa status, race/ethnicity, marital status, children under and over the age of six, and type of physical disability(ies), if any.

Educational: Field, degree received (month and year), and full or part-time college attendance in the five months preceding the survey. Graduate school status in 1993 is available by field and sex for bachelor's graduates and for 1991 and 1992 master's graduates.

Employment: Employment status, restrictions (if any) on job search, and reasons for being unemployed and not seeking. Employed in S/E or not, and, if not, reason why. Job characteristics of employed respondents include type of employer, code for type of activity, code for second job (if any), primary and secondary activities, and coded job specialty. Basic salary and period it covers, years of professional experience, self identification from degree, and employment codes. Government support for work and agency. Special questions on energy-related employment.

• AVAILABILITY

Characteristics of Recent Science and Engineering Graduates: 1990 (NSF 90-305). Floppy disks of tables are available. *Characteristics of Recent College Graduates: 1993*, forthcoming.

APPENDIX B

BASIC DESIGN PARAMETERS OF A LONGITUDINAL TRACKING SYSTEM FOR DOCTORAL STUDENTS

INTRODUCTION

In his 1988 report, Peter Ewell introduced some basic principles and techniques that institutions might use to construct a student tracking system, focusing on the need to collect accurate and detailed institution-specific information on student retention, persistence, and enrollment behavior using a "cohort tracking" model. The output of the longitudinal student record system can be a set of reports for institutional and external use.

Although it is beyond the purview of this study to introduce a specific student tracking system for doctoral-granting institutions, it is possible to draw from Ewell and others[1] in describing the general features of a longitudinal tracking record for students enrolled in Ph.D. programs in the sciences and humanities which individual institutions might modify. The purpose of this section is to outline the key features of a system for tracking.

PURPOSE OF THE TRACKING SYSTEM

The purpose of a longitudinal tracking system for graduate students is to construct a data base that provides a comprehensive picture of student progress through advanced degree work. The system should permit the analysis of variables contributing to successful and unsuccessful completion of doctoral studies. The cohort survival model (Ewell 1988; Zwick 1991; Bowen and Rudenstine 1992) lends itself to this type of analysis, but it requires the construction of discrete files for entering cohorts of students. These files are the heart of the tracking system.

DATA TO BE COLLECTED

The first issue in constructing a longitudinal tracking system is the definition of who will be included in the system. At the graduate level, a tracking system might (1) include all students admitted to and enrolled for credit in Ph.D. granting programs, (2)

---

[1]Other institutional researchers whose work has the potential to contribute to the design of a longitudinal student tracking system include Glover and Wilcox (1992), Nerad and Cerny (1991), Ehrenberg (1991), Tinto (1991), Tuckman, Coyle, and Bae (1989), and Zwick and Braun (1988).

track students over all terms whether they are enrolled or not, and (3) exclude students explicitly enrolled in terminal master's degree programs.

A cohort of students consists of all those who first enroll in a degree program on a given date. At any future date, this cohort can be divided into four types of students:

(1) those who have completed the degree;

(2) those who have officially left the program without completing;

(3) those who are still enrolled in the program; and

(4) those who have "stopped out" and may return.

Over time, students move from groups (3) and (4) into groups (1) and (2). At some arbitrary date (e.g., eight years later), completion and attrition rates can be calculated based on the number of students in groups (1) and (2). Unfortunately, students at some institutions may remain indefinitely in groups (3) and (4), and researchers will need to decide whether to create a third category for these "non-completers" or include them in the attrition rate.

Comprehensive tracking of graduate students will occur across a number of diverse graduate units (e.g., programs, departments, colleges) within an institution. To design and mount an effective student tracking system at the doctoral level, an institutionally based committee or graduate office would be needed to provide data managers with specific information about important differences in the graduate programs that must be reflected in longitudinal student records. For example, does the doctoral program include a master's degree requirement on the way to the doctorate?

The data elements actually included in a longitudinal tracking system will include a minimal set of information about a student as well as optional information. Some elements will be determined by institutional information needs as well as reporting requirements imposed by external agencies, such as state and federal governments. The elements listed in the text box on the following page are offered for purposes of illustration without regard to other reporting requirements.[2]

REPORTS

A longitudinal tracking system can be used to develop several types of reports. Through manipulation of the data set, cohort analyses can be conducted, yielding the following types of derived measures:

- number of students in a cohort
- number/percent of students earning master's degrees by a particular semester
- number/percent of students admitted to doctoral candidacy in a particular semester
- number/percent of students in attendance in a semester (full-time or part-time or terminated)

In addition, the data base can be used to develop prescriptive reports which assist planners and institutional researchers to document variables contributing to attrition, such as the nature and timing of student

---

[2]Coker and Feidel (1991) report that increasing emphasis on the assessment of institutional effectiveness has stimulated many campuses to examine existing data sources, surveys, and reports before proceeding to develop new measures.

FIXED DATA ELEMENTS

Admissions Characteristics

· name of student
· student ID number
· baccalaureate institution
· year of baccalaureate
· undergraduate grade point average
· GRE (verbal, quantitative, subject) scores
· entry semester into Ph.D. program
· transfer student (from)

Demographic Characteristics

· gender
· race/ethnic identification
· date of birth
· physical disabilities

VARIABLE DATA ELEMENTS

Demographic Characteristics

· citizenship
· number of dependents
· marital status

Enrollment Characteristics by Semester

· credits completed
· grade point average
· type of student support
· attendance status (full-time, part-time, on leave)

Degree Program Characteristics by Semester

· field/subfield
· department/academic unit
· advisor
· probationary status (if applicable)
· master's degree awarded (optional)
· admitted to candidacy
· dissertation committee (chair and members)
· doctoral degree awarded

---

support; family status; race or gender; access to faculty as advisors and/or dissertation committee chairs; and antecedent variables, such as the type/prestige of the baccalaureate institution.

REFERENCES

Bowen, William G., and Neil L. Rudenstine
1992　*In Pursuit of the PhD.* Princeton, NJ: Princeton University Press.

Coker, D., and J. Feidel
1991　"The Data Collection Matrix Model." *Research in Higher Education* 32(1): 71-81.

Ehrenberg, Ronald G.
1991　"Academic Labor Supply." In *Economic Challenges in Higher Education, Part 2*, edited by Charles T. Clotfelter, Ronald G. Ehrenberg, Malcolm Getz, and John J. Siegfried. Chicago, IL: University of Chicago Press.

Ewell, Peter
1988　*Establishing a Longitudinal Student Tracking System: An Implementation Handbook.* Boulder, CO: National Center for Higher Education.

Glover, Robert H., and Jerry Wilcox
1992　"An Interactive Model for Studying Student Retention." *AIR Professional File* 44 (Spring).

Nerad, Maresi, and Joseph Cerny
1991　"From Facts to Action: Expanding the Educational Role of the Graduate Division. *Communicator* (May Special Edition). Washington, DC: Council of Graduate Schools.

Tinto, Vincent
1991   "Toward a Theory of Graduate Persistence." Paper presented at the annual meeting of the American Educational Research Association, Chicago, Illinois.

Tuckman, Howard P., Susan Coyle, and Yupin Bae
1989   "The Lengthening of Time to Completion of the Doctorate Degree." *Research in Higher Education* 30: 503-16.

Zwick, Rebecca
1991   *An Analysis of Graduate School Careers in Three Universities: Differences in Attainment Patterns Across Academic Programs and Demographic Groups.* Princeton, NJ: Educational Testing Service.

Zwick, Rebecca, and Henry I. Braun
1988   *Methods for Analyzing the Attainment of Graduate School Milestones: A Case Study.* GRE Board Professional Report No. 86-3P. Princeton, NJ: Educational Testing Service.